John Kilham Porter

Guiteau Trial

Closing Speech to the Jury of John K. Porter of New York

John Kilham Porter

Guiteau Trial

Closing Speech to the Jury of John K. Porter of New York

ISBN/EAN: 9783337156299

Printed in Europe, USA, Canada, Australia, Japan

Cover: Foto ©Suzi / pixelio.de

More available books at **www.hansebooks.com**

GUITEAU TRIAL.

CLOSING SPEECH TO THE JURY

OF

JOHN K. PORTER,

OF NEW YORK,

IN THE CASE OF

CHARLES J. GUITEAU,

The Assassin of President Garfield,

WASHINGTON, JANUARY 23, 1882.

NEW YORK:
JOHN POLHEMUS, Printer, 102 Nassau Street.
1882.

GUITEAU TRIAL.

CLOSING SPEECH TO THE JURY
—OF—
JOHN K. PORTER,
OF NEW YORK,

In the case of CHARLES J. GUITEAU, the Assassin of President Garfield, Washington, January 23, 1882.

MONDAY, January 23, 1882.

The court met at ten o'clock; counsel for Government and accused being present.

Argument.

MR. PORTER. If it please your honor, gentlemen of the jury. In the infirmity of my own health, for I share your weariness, I proceed as well as I can to discharge the duty imposed upon me. Having been ill for over a week, the consequence of exposure to not only the confinement here, which we have shared with you, but also to labors out of court for over two months, I feared that I might have to abandon the attempt to address you at all. But the nature of the duty imposed upon me, not by my own seeking or procurement, is such that I should feel, as if I were almost an accessory after the fact to the prisoner's crime, if I omitted to say what my strength will permit, to aid you in reaching a just conclusion.

Gentlemen, I am sorry to say that thus far, unavoidably, the trial has been conducted and controlled to an unusual extent by the prisoner and his counsel, Mr. Scoville. Everybody has been arraigned, everybody denounced, everybody interrupted at their will. I have received notice from both of these two Guiteaus, that I am to be interrupted now; that I am to be permitted to utter nothing which each or either of those gentlemen, appearing as joint counsel in the case, may happen to disapprove. I believe, nevertheless, that what I think it necessary to say *will be said*, whatever obstacles they choose to interpose. It will be submitted in no rhetorical form, but with the earnestness and directness with which, if I were sitting by your own hearthstones, and reviewing the case in the spirit of perfect frankness and sincerity on your part and on mine, we should wish to discuss it. I deal only with the evidence, the facts, the issues and the law, as declared by the court. Of course you remember that this defence was begun with a two-days' opening speech, based upon an imaginary case, and which the counsel could not have supposed to be the one which was to come before you for judgment. The purpose was obvious. The opening counsel knew, what we did not—that he proposed to make the trial a very long one. It was important that you should begin the hearing, with impressions fixed by two days' iteration and re-iteration, in favor of the prisoner and against the Government. The trial proceeded. You heard the evidence, and much of it more than two months ago. You heard it, too, amid clamor, objections, interruption, vituperation and blasphemy. It was not the most favorable form in which to listen intelligently, or to remember perfectly, where you had no opportunity of making notes of the evidence, and were compelled to rely upon your memory, for that which is contained in these volumes, embracing some 2,200 pages, closely printed in Government type, and equal in ordinary print to nearly 5,000 pages. The prisoner's counsel knew that you could not, under such circumstances, recall each particular fact that impressed you at the time. Of course, too, they knew that at the close of the trial, much would be indistinctly recalled, and that it would be easy to confound statements and impressions made in the opening speech, with the actual facts established by the proofs.

On our side you have been addressed just two days, bating an hour and a half. One half hour of that time was made up by the eloquent opening speech of Mr. Corkhill. Nine days have been occupied in behalf of the prisoner, and seven of those days, since Mr. Davidge closed his able, eloquent and compact argument. I must say in justice to the prisoner, that of the three arguments which have been made by him and his associate counsel, the one most free from objection was that delivered by him. Aside from the impiousness of his allegations, habitual with him through the previous stages of the trial, it was free, at least, from the singular misstatements and perversions of testimony, abounding in the arguments of his two associates.

I wish to recall your attention to this case as it is, upon the evidence; and inasmuch as I am publicly warned that I will not be permitted to speak what the prisoner or his counsel disapprove, I shall be under the necessity of referring you, in greater detail than usual, to the actual and controlling evidence in the cause. As to anything beyond that, gentlemen of the jury, you need expect nothing from me, and certainly the assassin and his defenders need fear nothing from me. My relations to the case are simply those imposed by plain and manifest duty, under the full conviction, from the proof, confirmed by the declarations and oath of the party accused, that the interests of public justice demand, that the crafty and deliberate murderer of President Garfield shall not be discharged from the dock, until he is convicted and under sentence of death; that he should then pass to the sterner shackles of the murderer's cell, there to invoke the mercy of that God who sometimes, as we believe, pardons guilt, but not the guilt which spares no human being. The prisoner did not spare President Garfield, though he acknowledged that the victim was a good man, whom he was merely transferring by murder to paradise. He did not spare the wife, who by simply leaning upon the President's arm, saved his life on the 18th of June, and who, as he swears, if she had leaned upon his arm on the 2d of July would have saved him then. He did not spare the mother whom the son so honored, that yielding to the deep feeling of filial love and gratitude, on his inauguration day, the first act after he kissed the Bible in taking his constitutional oath, was to press his lips to those of that aged lady, in the presence of the assembled multitude. The assassin spared no one then. He spares no one now. A murderer at heart then, he is a murderer at heart now, and he has established by his oath as a witness, his own frozen, merciless, and unrelenting malice, restrained by nothing but his crouching and abject cowardice.

Gentlemen, you have witnessed the bearing of this man on the trial. *The ordinary presumption of innocence is repelled by his own oath*, impudently avowing his guilt, and imputing the blame to the Almighty. Let me ask you, whether, if he were now unshackled, and fully assured of the efficacy of the mock defense of insanity as his shield and protection—with that bulldog pistol in his grasp—he would not have put a summary end to this trial when, the other day, his honor, in his own personal views of propriety and duty, prohibited him from making a last speech—when the judge, who had been the object of his fulsome and offensive praise, became at once the mark of his fiendlike hate—and when the assassin, disregarding for the moment, in the violence of his temper, even his own dependence for the time on the jurist who had shown such liberal clemency, warned even him, that such a decision would compel him to erase from the record he had made for this people and for after times, the commendation he had kindly bestowed on the judge, and to send his name blackened down the course of history. Do you believe that the prisoner who, on his own showing, shot a good and upright man; who dogged him at night; who went to church to murder him; who lay in wait in front of his home to butcher him—if he had felt secure of immunity, would not at the time of that decision, instead of threatening his honor's name with infamy, have sent one of these cartridges to his heart? That is for you to judge, with the scene fresh in your remembrance. Do you think, when my friend Mr. Davidge was delivering that masterly, earnest and conclusive argument against him, bringing home his guilt as a murderer, if he had held that charged pistol in the dock, feeling safe, as he professes to have felt in the case of President Garfield, in relying on his assumed insanity, that he would have paused to practice, before he had aimed at him another of the cartridges which he drove through the backbone of the President? Do you think the man, who when one of your number was bowed in grief beneath the shadow of death, which had darkened the light of his home, passed out in front of the jury, uttering that ribald boast over the plaster cast that was to transmit his name to after times, would not even then, if it had occurred to him that he could *safely* serve a purpose of his own, and terminate this trial, have pointed that pistol at the juror? True, as in President Garfield's case, it would have been in no spirit of ill-will to the juror, but simply of good-will to himself. It would have given him a few more months of life, and increased the chances of final escape, through the difficulty of again impaneling an impartial jury. The prisoner showed his idea of mercy to others, when, during the trial, in one of his brutal outbursts of passion, impiously and blasphemously, he menaced an act of God which should end the case and avert a conviction. Gentlemen, this is the man of whom we are to speak, and in whose behalf his counsel, with such touching pathos, invokes merciful and tender consideration at your hands. The evidence shows him to have been cunning, crafty, and remorseless, utterly selfish from his youth up, low and brutal in his instincts, inordinate in his love of notoriety; eaten up by a lust for money which has gnawed into his soul like a cancer; a beggar, a hypocrite, a canter, a swindler, a lawyer who, with many years of practice in two great cities never won a cause, and you know why; a man who has left in every State through which he passed, a trail of knavery, fraud, and imposition; a man who has lived at the expense of others, and when he succeeded in getting possession of their funds, appropriated them to his own private use, in breach of every honorable obligation and every professional trust; a man capable of mimicking the manners and aping the bearing of a gentleman; who bought at pawnbrokers' shops the cast-off clothing, for which he paid only when his credit elsewhere was exhausted; and then, with his plausibility of religious cant, his studied skill as an actor, his unscrupulous self-commendation, drifting about from State to State, professing to be engaged in the work of the Lord; a man, who as a lawyer, collected doubtful debts by dogging the debtor, pocketed the money as against his clients, and chuckled over their credulity in trusting him; a man who pawned counterfeit watches as gold, to eke out a professional livelihood; a man capable even of endeavoring to blast the name of the woman with whom he had slept for years, and whom he acknowledges to have been a true and faithful wife; capable of palming himself off upon the public, upon Christian associations, upon Christian churches from city to city, as a pure and upright man, though he had spent years in shameless fornication; a man who afterwards, when he wished to get rid of his wife, consulted the commandments of God, and reading "Thou shalt not commit adultery," went out and committed it with a prostitute. He thought it needful that his wife should be "removed." Fortunately for her, it did not come to the necessity of the *form* of "removal" which he applied to President Garfield. He was content with that which he could procure for himself by a *safer* crime, and afterwards appeared before the judicial referee as a witness to estabish the marriage, and, as the record shows, produced the prostitute to prove the adultery. He is proved by his own witness to have been so void of all honor, so possessed of the spirit of diabolism, that he was capable at the age of eighteen of stealing up behind his own father, giving him a cowardly blow when seated at his own table, and relying upon the fact that he was then a larger and stronger man than the father, as the latter rose, exchanged blow after blow with him, and when the old gentleman by a fortunate stroke drew blood on his face, the son at once surrendered—a coward, then as now. The spirit in which at forty he fired at Garfield, was the spirit in which at eighteen he struck his father from behind. This too, bear in mind, was over a year before he entered the Oneida Community, to which Mr. Scoville refers the date of his pretended insanity. It was seventeen years before the menace to Mrs. Scoville, with the ax, in 1876 ; before which time, as she *finally* testifies, *she never had any thought that he was not in his right mind.*

That was the occasion, when he lifted his ax against a lady, who, however unfortunate her present position, as his sister and Mr. Scoville's wife, has my sincere sympathy and respect, for her thankless devotion to this brother from childhood up. For her fidelity to him here, I have nothing to say but words of kindness and regard. This is the same man, who afterward and on another occasion, illustrated the same spirit of malignity, by striking his own brother.

Mr. SCOVILLE. Judge Porter, one moment. If the court please, I want to call attention to one thing on page 465, where at the bottom of the page Mrs. Scoville said that she visited him at Ann Arbor and I was trying to reason with him and was laboring with him in regard to giving up those ideas, " I thought it would be the ruin of him if he went to that place, and I told him so ; and I wanted him to continue with his studies and go on quietly, as a young man should, and let all that stuff go. I could not influence him a particle. At last I made up my mind that the man was crazy, from the way he acted and talked to me ; and I told my uncle that I should give no more attention to trying to turn him from that idea ;" that was when he was at Ann Arbor, before he went to the Oneida Community at all.

Mr. PORTER. So I understood her ; but that was on the examination by *her* husband and *his* brother-in-law, uncorrected by her cross-examination. Mrs. Scoville was an honest woman ; and however biased she might naturally be by her feelings and affections, she did not refrain on cross-examination from frankly admitting the truth as it was. I have no doubt that she thought these boyish ideas were crazy, at the time, crazy in the popular sense ; that it was a crazy thing in him to do what his father wanted him to do; that it was a crazy thing in him to believe what she did not believe;

that it was a crazy thing in him to regard John H. Noyes more favorably than she did. But we are dealing with the question of *actual* insanity. That is the question for you to consider. And at page 472, after relating the ax story of 1876, she testifies in these words:

"*I had never had any thought of him before, that he was not in his right mind.*"

Thus much for the interruption. I am glad it occurred. It enables me to verify the fact of which I was speaking. How natural was her feeling. Not knowing his intense depravity, she might well ask, can this be the sane act of my brother, who owes me so much, whom I have befriended from childhood, whom I have induced my husband to befriend, to liberate from jail, to deliver from the Oneida Community, to furnish a roof to cover his head, when no other roof in Christendom was at his command? Can it be that he, merely because I raise a stick of wood, but with no intention of striking him with it, is ready to lift his ax against my life? Well might she be alarmed. True it was an alarm which soon subsided; but *we* know what *she* did not, that the menace to her was in keeping with the assault on his father, from whose table he received his daily bread, and beneath whose roof he slept. He denies the truth of the ax story, told by his sister; but when his oath and hers come in collision, you will have no difficulty in determining which of them is to be believed. Truth and falsehood never harmonize. Mr. Reed, appreciating the utter folly of the contradiction of Mrs. Scoville by the prisoner, offers the lame apology that his client had probably *forgotten* it. What! forgotten that five years ago, at his sister's own house, he had menaced her life, and menaced it with an uplifted ax! That is like his first address to the American people, in which he justified the killing of the President as a political act, and *forgot* to plead the Divine inspiration and command, which he now sets up as his sole defense. That first address was dated *eighteen days before the assassination.* I read from page 216 of the evidence:

"In the President's madness he has wrecked the grand old Republican party, and *for this he dies.*" So in his *second* address, delivered to Mr. Reynolds *sixteen days after the assassination,* the Divine command was *still forgotten.* I read from page 1109, what he there says of the murder:

"It was *my own conception and execution,* and whether right or wrong I take the entire responsibility of it.

"CHARLES GUITEAU."

Astounded as he was on learning from Reynolds, that men of all parties united in regarding his crime with loathing and abhorrence, he wrote another address on the following day, in which he says, at page 1118:

"*My sole object* in removing General Garfield was to unite the contending factions of the Republican party, and keep the government in their control."

Even in his then desperate condition, he had "*forgotten*" the Divine command, but there is a faint dawn in a single phrase, of the Oneida Community idea of inspiration, stolen from the "*Berean*" of John H. Noyes:

"I have got the inspiration *worked out of me.*"

Gentlemen, we have seen what this man was at the age of eighteen, when he fought his father. We have seen what he was at the age of thirty-five, when he raised an ax against his sister. Let us see what he was two years before he murdered the President, as his character is revealed to us by his own witness and brother, John W. Guiteau. At that time the prisoner was thirty-eight years of age. His brother, a worthy and respectable citizen of Boston, had from time to time befriended him. The prisoner called at his office, and John kindly remonstrated with him against his habit of deceiving and imposing upon boarding-house keepers. The prisoner proposed to fight, but John declined, and requested him to leave the office. As he was going out, he impudently told John, *he was a thief.* Irritated by the epithet, he gave him a slight slap with his open hand. The prisoner turned and gave him a blow in the face, for which, John says, he respected him, for he did not suppose he had so much pluck. You will remember that the record discloses no other instance, in which he ever struck a first blow at anybody, his own father included, except from behind. He relapsed, however, at once into his usual cowardice, and though John was the smaller man, he tells you, at page 497, that he hustled him out of the office *very roughly*—"took him by the collar very forcibly and heartily, and *threw him down stairs.*"

The next meeting of the two brothers was in the cell of the prisoner, after he had waylaid and murdered the President.

We next find him, so far as we are enabled to trace him in the evidence, indulging in the same spirit of cowardly malignity and violence, when, after six weeks of cool and wicked deliberation, freshly reminded of the claims of President Garfield upon the country for which he had fought bravely and manfully in war, and which he had eminently honored in peace; that country of which he, differing in that respect from many of his associates, had sought the pacification; that country, in whose behalf, as one of the leaders of the American bar, he made the first great argument which, in conjunction with that of Judge Black, moved the Supreme Court of the United States to a decision, sustaining the policy of pacification and ending the strife of war. That statesman, who had been so long in the service of the country, and coming out of it with a name so untarnished, that when he was not even a candidate for office, he was taken up by a great party, and nominated to the place, to which no strict and rigid Republican could have at that time been elected; whose unforeseen nomination was taken up with one accord by the American people, and through the spontaneous recognition of the integrity, the ability, the patriotism, the fidelity, and the honor of the man, through such aid as he received from the Democratic party, without which he never could have been elected, was elevated to the Presidency, by a vote so clear and so strong that all the people said, amen; and this miserable and selfish rogue is for six weeks, and, as he says, without the slightest honest ground for personal malice toward him, plotting and plotting, with no counsel, except that of the fiend of darkness who prompted the suggestion, plotting, plotting through those long weeks the murder of the President. Is there any dispute about this? He swears to it, as a witness in his own cause. He complains that I call him an assassin. I called him an assassin, from the moment he swore he was one, and so do you. The law calls him an assassin. I had no reserve in treating him as a murderer from the moment he, swearing in his own behalf, said, I did commit a so-called murder, and intended to commit it.

Again, what do you find in the other evidence to throw light upon the acknowledged fact. If you take his oath, flatly contradicted by almost every witness he has called to the stand, in one particular or another—which would itself condemn him as wholly unworthy of credit—accepting his oath, for two weeks after *he*, not the Deity, formed the conception of murder, he knelt every night at the foot of God, with whom, he is now, as he says, very well satisfied, *so far*, but no farther—begged to have him work a miracle, in order to advise him whether after all this was not an inspiration of the devil; and, as the Deity worked *no miracle*, he concluded that the murder which he meditated was an *inspiration* of God; and then, from the first day of June, was so settled in his purpose of murder, so fixed, that he would have butchered him on the first opportunity, although he knew that the next minute he would himself be made the victim of just popular indignation. Yet, though he had so made up his mind on the first of June, you find him declaring to Mr. Brooks *at midnight of the day of the murder*, that for six weeks he had meditated the assassination, and for six weeks had been struggling and agonizing and praying to God to deliver him from this diabolic temptation.

Praying to God! If you could conceive of a prayer to God from this prisoner, I am sure you cannot conceive of one that he should be *delivered from his purpose* of cold-blooded and deliberate murder of the President, who had refused him the consulship at Paris. He tells you he was praying from night to night, and from day to day. We have information of a few prayers he has made. The most earnest he ever made in his life, was that *to you*, on Saturday, with tears unbecoming manhood, to grant him a safe deliverance and pronounce him a lunatic. It is said that he made some prayers at the Christian Association meetings and at the lecture room of the Rev. Dr. MacArthur. I believe it is pretended even, that he prayed at Mr. Moody's meetings. There he was an usher, and nothing more. In all the record of his life, aside from this, surrounded as he was by boarders, by guests, by brothers and sisters, by Reed and Scoville and Mrs. Scoville, there is no record of any prayer to God, if he made even one. Do you really think his knees would even now show the unhealed scars of his later prayers?

The PRISONER (Interjecting excitedly). I pray every night of my life. If you would pray some you would be a better man. You wouldn't be here for blood money.

Mr. PORTER. (Continuing.) Do you believe that he is a man of God and a man of prayer? It is the pretence of a perjured and forsworn witness, on which this defense rests. Has he been in a prayer-making mood at any time, until he came before you as a witness, since he has been in this court-room? You have been compelled to live with this man, two and a half months of your life, each man of you. You have been imprisoned, isolated from your families, from your wives, from your children, held together as if you were criminals, because the law required your seclusion. Each of you twelve has been confined, during the last two and a half months of your lives, not for any wrong of yours, but for that man's act. He is the culprit, and so much of the lives which God gave you has been cut off, and by him. You little thought when that bullet was flattened against the spine of President Garfield, that you were to suffer a share of the penalty, and that you were to have so much stricken from your own lives. That has happened to each of you. True, it is in obedience to the mandate of the law; but it was through his wrong. You have performed a painful and a bitter duty. One of you has performed it under the gloom of the shadow of death. That others have not, though equally exposed, is due to the merciful providence in which you trust, though the prisoner does not, except in mockery. He tells you, gentlemen, that he did pray; that he prayed for six weeks. What for? If he had made up his mind so fixedly on the 1st of June, that he would have murdered the President, though he were to perish the next instant, what was he praying about? He tells Brooks that he was praying to God, as his ultimate judge, to know, if what of murder he had been premeditating was right or wrong. Not a word of *inspiration*, not a word of *God's command*. All that he had forgotten; and yet you remember he swears that his insanity came on the 1st of June, and that it left him within an hour after he murdered the president. From that hour he has been a sane man. Strangely enough, when he recovered his sanity, he remembered all the incidents of his insanity, and he remembers, among other things, that after he made up his mind unchangeably, to murder the president, on the 1st of June, he was praying to God, down to the very day of the assassination, to know whether he was doing his duty or not. I am reminding you of these things, gentlemen, in order to connect with them some of the other circumstances, which have already flashed across your minds. This man who believed, or professed to believe, that the God who spoke to Moses, and the Saviour who summoned Paul to replace the Judas among the twelve who had been false to his trust, tells you on his own oath, that he meditated the means with cool deliberation ; that *he* contrived beforehand his infamous partisan vindication ; that *he* prepared the papers which were to justify him as a Stalwart, before God and man ; and that *he revised* his inspired book of Truth and *altered it*. What ! Alter the immediate and direct inspiration of God ? Blotting out hell in this book, as a deliberate preliminary to the murder of President Garfield, and substituting the milder term perdition ! Does inspiration need *alteration*, by the very man who received it direct from the Deity ? Making his preparations for the crime, engaged in the work of the Lord, borrowing the money on false pretenses with which to execute that work, representing that he wanted it to pay board bills, and getting fifteen dollars, ten dollars of which were appropriated to the purpose of murder !

Again, we find the same man practicing with his pistol on the river side. What for ? Bear in mind, gentlemen, he has told you again and again that the question and the only question for you is, " Did the Deity fire that shot, or did I ? If I did, there is no punishment that would be too quick and severe for me. If the Deity, you cannot try Him for it." No, you cannot.

But *who was it* that was practicing, in order to make sure of a deadly aim, the Deity, or the prisoner in the dock ? Who shot at those osiers, who sent them swaying down as Garfield did ? Who hit them ? Who fired twenty times, in order to accustom himself to the report of the pistol, to the end that it should not stun him while he murdered the President, for he had things to say immediately after, which were all prepared ? Who was it, who went to the depot on the 18th of June, with his hand in his hip-pocket, his pistol well wiped and cleaned ; this, too, after a good night's sleep, a refreshing morning bath, and an hour of practicing at the river bank; lying in wait afterwards to murder the president, waiting until he and his wife came in, and for once, for once and once only, even his malice was overcome, and he could not muster the courage to pull that trigger. This was two weeks after God had issued the peremptory command to murder President Garfield, and no danger to himself could avert his homicidal act. There is no diabolism so complete on this side of the infernal regions, but there are still some remaining twinges of conscience. He shrank, coward as he was, against murdering the man, while his wife was leaning upon his arm. He faltered afterwards on a second occasion from murdering him, because, as it happened, he had with him his two children, holding their father by the hand.

The tears, and the only tears, he is known to have shed from boyhood, were for himself. The only evidences of humanity he has disclosed on this trial were, that he spared General Garfield when his wife was present, and spared him when her children were by; and, gentlemen, my firm belief is that the reason he assigns is as false as anything else he swears to. He knew that if he had fired *then* into Garfield's back, there would be no opportunity to appeal to Stalwarts. The whole army of the United States could not have protected him. If he had committed the murder *then*, what would have become of the plea of insanity? He knew that no force that General Sherman had at his command, could have prevented the American people, or at least those who had access to him, from tearing him limb from limb. There are occasions when human nature overrides the restraints of law, forgets and ignores them. He did not care to bring that terrible horror upon him. He was a cringing coward. On the occasion of the murder, there was, as he says, a Cabinet meeting, consisting of the President and Mr. Blaine; but on the other occasion, when Mrs. Garfield was upon the arm of the President, there were those attendant upon her, infirm as she was—making in his eyes a crowd around—there was no probable chance for that bull-dog to do its work, and allow him to get out of that depot alive. This man has *no malice*, you understand. He thought it would be an excellent place *at church* to remove the President. He would lift him right from the pew to Paradise. He had a great regard for President Garfield's soul; he felt intensely in his behalf. He thought he was unhappy among these politicians, and he would elevate him at once to a better sphere. He saw it would not do to shoot through the doorway, not because it would endanger other people's lives, but because *it endangered his own life*. Well, he stays after the President leaves, and goes around to the window, having observed the pew and the seat of the President. He looks through, to see where he could stand and where he could shoot. It was that little church in which the President worshiped God, whom this man never worshiped; that little church, where without ostentation the President went with his friends, according to his creed, not according to yours or mine. He went there the simple citizen of the United States, as an unpretentious creature of God, conscious of sin, and bowing in reverence to that holy name. Guiteau thought there he could shoot him—there and well; *shoot him safely*. He would wait for him until next Sunday. He had his pistol in his pocket. "Next Sunday I will do it." Next Sunday came. God, who, as he says, inspired him to murder, so ordered it, that the President the next Sunday worshiped at Long Branch, where his sick wife was, and the murderer was baffled again. On the night before the actual assassination, this man, in perfect health, with good sleep, with good appetite, who had been discussing with Dr. Shippen at Mrs. Grant's table for a month, the various questions of interest, the revision of the New Testament, the situation of affairs at Albany, the prospect of extrication from the dead lock, had been turned out for defrauding his landlady, and had gone to the Riggs House, where, of course, he never paid his board, and never intended to, and then, as it was a very warm night, had gone out to relieve himself from the pressure of the heat. He went where? To Lafayette Square. Well, as he only went *to get cool*, of course he did not need his weapon of death, but by inadvertence he did put that bull-dog pistol into his pocket, carefully wrapped up in paper. There he watched and waited until President Garfield came out. There was a present opportunity. The Almighty ruler of the universe, as he impudently pretends, had commanded him to do the murderous act, an act from which he would not have refrained, if it had cost him his life the very next instant, and when, as he claims, the Almighty was urging him on to the deed, he held back. It was night; dark as that night on which he conceived the cold-blooded purpose of murder; dark as the night on which the devil first whispered into his ear the project of assassination. President Garfield came out to take an evening saunter alone; walked past him and went on to the house of Mr. Blaine. In the alley, this assassin was lying in wait, like an Indian in ambush. There was the armed murderer, and there his unconscious prey. "Why did you not shoot him when he went by? He was *alone*." "I did not feel like it." Here again was the shrinking of the coward. He was in a vacillating mood. This was a murder, not, as he says, from ill-will to General Garfield, but simply to make himself the idol of the Stalwart party, the Republican party, and the American people. If he did it when he was alone, nobody would know it was his act. If he did it in the dark, there would not be the notoriety which should attend President Garfield's death. Thus, through the cowardice and selfishness of the murderer, the President escaped for the time, unconscious that at that moment he held his life upon the mere tenure of Guiteau's will. The assassin controlled himself, simply because he thought it *better for himself;* but on reconsideration, while the President was in Mr. Blaine's house, he came to the conclusion, "I will do it, after all." He went back into the alley-way, and at first he would have had you believe it was a casual visit. In the end he admits that he was waiting for Garfield to come out; that he thrust his hand into his hip-pocket, drew out this pistol, with the means of taking five human lives, wiped it, tried it to see that it was in order, and held it in readiness for his victim. The President after a time came out. There is the assassin, hiding in the alley-way. There is the dark sky above. There is no human witness. It had occurred to him, undoubtedly, in the meanwhile, Even though there is nobody here, I can acknowledge the act tomorrow, and by timely retreat to-night secure myself against any outbreak of the mob. He evidently made up his mind to murder him when he came out. But when the President came, the Secretary of State was with him, arm in arm. Guiteau faltered. In a moment he could have been as near to him, as I am to your foreman. He had but to advance a few steps, and the deed would be done. Nobody would suspect him. He could have shot him in the back. But there was a restraining power above; there was a restraining power below. It had not yet been appointed in the providence of God, that this great crime should be consummated.

What does he do? He takes his cool observation. There are two men there. He came to kill but one, and that without a witness. He knows that he is an inexperienced marksman, having only practiced some twenty times in shooting, and he might not kill the President at the first shot, with time to kill Blaine afterwards. Who knew but Blaine might look back and seize him, or even in the righteous indignation of the occasion, lift his cane and strike him down. He thought on the whole, "It is a hot night; *I will take him alone.*" The President and Blaine go on. This ingenious lawyer, this keen office-seeking politician, considering the matter, thinks he had better eavesdrop a little, even though he does not care then to kill, and he creeps up behind them, and listens to their conversation. He finds that they are arm in arm, and that they are both gesticulating earnestly. This, he would have you believe, excited him to murder. Excited him to murder! Why, if God commanded it on the first of June, what need of such excitement? But he tells us that the murder was due to the political situation. He would not have killed him but for that. When he saw Blaine earnestly gesticulating, and the President putting his arm upon his shoulder and talking kindly with him, he knew then, though he had only suspected it before, that we were on the eve of a civil war, and "that the only thing that could be done to save the Republican party was to kill the President." He goes home. He has a good night's sleep. He forgets to tell us, when he is a witness on the stand, that it was a night of prayer, and that his knees were stiff with supplication through all these weeks. He slept well. He rose early in the morning, after having gone to bed at nine o'clock.

He dressed himself; he went to the depot; disposed of his papers, examined his pistol, and ascertained when the President was to leave. He had prepared everything. He put the address to the American people, in which he strangely forgets that God had commanded him to do this murder, in a place where it would reach Byron Andrews, felt for his letter to General Sherman, and arranged what? Plans for President Garfield's safety? Oh, no, no; Garfield was to be gently removed to Paradise. Plans for whose safety? *That of Charles Guiteau*, for which he tells you he cared nothing, nothing. He would have killed the President if he had known that he was to be torn in pieces that moment. He engages a hack to drive him out to the jail as his only place of refuge, and then, in the same spirit of personal vanity which led him to buy a white pistol rather than a plain one, because it would be more conspicuous on exhibition in the Patent Office, has his boots properly blacked, then goes to the water-closet, feels for his pistol, examines it, wipes it, replaces it; comes out and parades as a sentinel in front of the ladies' door; arranges all his plans; selects his station for the murder, within easy distance of the President's back, when he shall have passed in; listens to the conversation of the President and Secretary Blaine; is confirmed—he would have you believe it was by God—in the idea that it is his *his duty* to save the Republican party; steps quietly out of the way; allows them to pass in, *supposing himself to be unobserved*, and then in the presence of that Virginia girl, whom God sent there to witness and disclose the truth on this trial, sneaks up behind the President, pulls the trigger, though Secretary Blaine was by his side, sees that he does *not* fall, drives home the second bullet, sees that he *does* fall, and turns to escape. To escape where? To escape to the jail; and careful, in the very last moment, of his own safety, holds in his hand the letter to General Sherman, which shall instantly summon those to protect him, who were not at hand to protect the murdered President. He retreats to the door. He is intercepted by an officer. He is brought back flourishing his letter to General Sherman, his only idea of secure protection. He was right, for no sooner does he pass beyond that door, and is recognized as the man, than the cry rises, "Lynch him! hang the murderer!" He hurries the officers and they hurry him, closing around him, until this "gentleman," as Mr. Scoville calls him, this moral man, this truth-telling man, this man of God, this man of prayer, may be taken to the jail, protected by armed guards, such as would ordinarily resist the populace, but not perhaps in such an emergency, and he calls upon *the Government* to protect him, though it had not protected the President, whom he had accused, had tried, and sentenced, and had murdered. He has been very scrupulous, your honor, upon the question whether you had extended to him every right he has chosen to demand in this case, full constitutional protection, the largest freedom of speech, the perfect impartiality, which in his view was to consist in making all the decisions in his favor, in permitting him to dictate your charge, proposing now to have you modify your instructions after you have passed upon them. He was quite willing to escape to jail, but very averse to sitting in the dock, which he thinks a disparagement to a lawyer, a theologian, a politician, a man of God, a man of prayer, a patriot, a man whose name is to go on "resounding through all the ages."

Mr. SCOVILLE. If the Court please, I want to correct one thing in Judge Porter's statement of the evidence. At the bottom of page 170 this witness, Mrs. Ridgely, states what every one of the witnesses said substantially in relation to his conduct immediately after the shooting. Judge Porter says that he started to run away. I do not recollect a single witness who testified to that effect. I will read from the testimony of Mrs. Ridgely.

Mr. PORTER. I have not time for that.

Mr. DAVIDGE. All understand the motive of this, may it please your honor. I presume this is the beginning of a series of interruptions to the argument of my learned friend who is closing this case. It is for your honor to say whether you will permit this at all, and, if so, to what extent you will permit it. They have had an opportunity of commenting on the evidence; the jury have heard the evidence. If my friend, Judge Porter, should through accident, and it cannot happen in any other way, fall into error, there will be no difficulty in correcting that error without interruption on the part of these gentlemen. What I apprehend is, and I may as well state it frankly and openly, a studious system of interruptions, whereby it is hoped the force of the closing argument in this cause may be broken.

Mr. SCOVILLE. Gentlemen need not apprehend it at all, because there will be nothing of the kind. I waited until Judge Porter came to a pause, and simply wished to correct him by reference to the testimony. I am not disposed to interrupt at all so as to disconcert the gentleman. I simply want the testimony stated correctly.

Mr. DAVIDGE. I am very sure that Officer Kearney said that he caught the man going out of the door, and told him that he would not let him go out, that two pistol shots had been fired, and then put him under arrest. Are we to have a wrangle over the matter?

The COURT. No; I shall have no dispute over the effect of the evidence at all. If Judge Porter, in reading the evidence, makes a mistake, it is proper to correct him. But in stating his understanding of the effect of the evidence, I do not think he ought to be interrupted, because it will lead to a running debate.

Mr. DAVIDGE. It would be to deny the closing argument.

Mr. SCOVILLE. If Judge Porter states that a certain matter is shown by the evidence and it is not, I have a right to show it.

The COURT. If he reads the evidence and makes a mistake, I think you can correct him; but there should be no running debate over the correctness of his recollection.

Mr. SCOVILLE. If I cannot refer him right to the page, I will not say a word; I will not put my recollection against his in any case. What I refer to is simply this——

Mr. DAVIDGE. (Interposing.) I object; I want to know whether the argument is to be allowed in its integrity, or whether it is to be cut to pieces by interruption?

The COURT. No.

Mr. DAVIDGE. I agree with your honor that if Judge Porter makes a mistake in reading, they can refer to the record and put him right; but if Judge Porter does nothing more than state his recollection of the evidence, that is what Mr. Scoville has been doing for five days.

The COURT. That is so. The argument must not be cut up in that way. The jury will have to decide if there is a difference in the gentlemen about recollection. It is only where the testimony is read verbatim and a mistake made that it is proper to correct it.

Mr. Scoville. If the Court please, I merely wish to say this: If Judge Porter says, I do not care whether from his recollection or from referring to the evidence in detail, that a certain thing is a fact and shown by the evidence, and asserts it to be so to the jury, and I can refer to the testimony of that identical witness that it is not so, I claim the right to do it.

The Court. It must be a strong case in which that privilege can be given. It would lead to a running debate. You have had your say, and the jury must decide as to which is the correct representation of the testimony. It would not do to allow a regular debate to go on over the effect of the testimony.

Mr. Scoville. It is simply a question of a statement of fact; that is all. If the Court please, we have no opportunity whatever of correcting these things hereafter. I shall not interfere unless I consider it material and I am certain a misstatement has been made. I have simply wanted to get at the facts, and I do not desire to have the jury take the statements of counsel or my own statements. We have here a large mass of testimony. The jury cannot remember it. It may be that the argument should proceed without interruption. Whether that is so or not, I wish to state that counsel interrupted me one hundred and forty-five times, and I was perfectly content with it whenever a question of fact came in. That is the actual number of times. I did not object to it once.

Mr. Davidge. That was only where you were reading testimony.

Mr. Scoville. I have only interrupted the gentleman twice, and I shall not interrupt him at all unless I consider it material. I say it was not the testimony of a single witness——

The Court. (Interposing.) You cannot discuss that question in the middle of the argument.

Mr. Scoville. But I have a right to refer to the testimony.

Mr. Davidge. No one ever heard of such a practice.

The Court. No.

Mr. Scoville. I will refer you to the case of Mary Harris, when District Attorney Harrington attempted to misstate facts. To this Judge Bradley objected, and as the district attorney persisted, the Court told him that if he did not stop he would put him in charge of the United States marshal. I propose to have this question decided here as to whether Judge Porter shall go on and misrepresent facts to this jury.

Mr. Davidge. Your honor must see the purpose of this interruption; it must be apparent to all minds.

The Court. Let Judge Porter proceed. We cannot have a running discussion in the midst of the argument. Proceed, judge.

The Prisoner. I refer the matter to the jury. I guess they understand that evidence about as good as any one. The policeman seized me simultaneously with my putting up my pistol.

Mr. PORTER. This man appeals to you to violate your oaths in the face of what he swears to. He swears to facts which prove him a deliberate, wicked, malicious murderer. He swears to facts which prove that he was a coward; that he did not commit the crime without providing for his own personal safety. These precautions were well and wisely taken. They were steps which probably would not have occurred to one other criminal in the United States. I do not think that one other man, in meditating the murder of the President, would have gone so far as to suppose that he could command the Federal Army for the purpose of shielding him from the danger to which he had exposed himself. They say he was crazy. Yet he judged rightly. He knew what that murder meant. *It meant political revolution.* It was committed with that view. It meant a change of administration. It meant, according to his ideas, the sweeping out of those who were in office, and the introduction of those who should owe their elevation to power to him. He evidently believed that he was a fair type of mankind, that they were all masked, that they were all playing a part, and that whatever promoted their own interests, they would defend and reward. Believing that, which the tempter had whispered in his ear, he took the steps which he thought would save him from the instant punishment, that he was conscious of deserving, confident that in due time those benefited by his act would come to his rescue.

The PRISONER. This is a good time for me to say that I am the only man that has not been benefited by the new administration.

Mr. PORTER. He is not benefited by it. He will not be benefited by it, until the day comes when the law shall speak and he will be silent. Then, if he be like the man he murdered, a good man, worthy to be removed to Paradise, he will inherit the benefit which rewards the just. He evidently *expected* to be benefited. Has not he told you again and again, that he was to be benefited in the advertisement and sale of his book ; second, in the recognition he should receive for elevating President Arthur to the successorship, which he claims to have been his act ; third, the pardon which he now probably expects, even in view of these facts, from President Arthur for the offence, of which he is now in peril of conviction. He professes to believe that the government counsel are in conspiracy to convict him. His pretense is that we suppressed evidence in his favor. His actual ground of complaint is that we *did not suppress* the evidence which crushes him to the earth, if you concur with us as to its effect.

The PRISONER. How about that note-book which was suppressed ?

Mr. PORTER. Gentlemen, it is perhaps well that, among the multitudinous falsehoods and misstatements, which for the last two months we have heard from the prisoner and his counsel, a brief reference be made to some of them. I do not propose to deal with Mr. Scoville or Mr. Reed. This case looms immeasurably too high, to allow us, in the final argument to the jury, to bring them into the discussion, except where it becomes necessary incidentally in considering the guilt or innocence of Guiteau. But it has been asserted by him and by Mr. Scoville, that the counsel for the government have been acting in this matter on the pledge of extraordinary fees.

Gentlemen, it is well, merely because the purpose of the allegations was to affect your minds unfavorably, to put a quietus upon these statements. Colonel Corkhill is the United States attorney for this District, and has been so for years. He has very important and responsible duties to discharge. Where he has reason to believe that crime has been committed, it is his duty to make investigation and to present proper cases to the consideration of the grand jury. If they, on investigation, find them to be cases calling for indictment, it is the duty of the United States attorney to have them submitted, in due course of law, to a petit jury for determination. Colonel Corkhill, with every citizen of Washington, and almost every citizen of the United States, was shocked by the telegraphic intelligence that the President had been assassinated. It was his business to ascertain by whom. He did so. *It turned out that he made no mistake.* There was but one man, among the fifty millions of Americans on that day, who was capable of shooting President Garfield in the back, and that man was Charles Julius Guiteau.

The PRISONER. He was the only man who had Divine authority to do it. *A great many wanted to do it.*

Mr. PORTER. It was his business, as United States Attorney, to ascertain the circumstances of the murder. He did it. He consulted, as was his duty on so momentous an occasion, with the then Attorney-General of the United States.

The first thing was to learn the exact facts, and they could only be ascertained in detail from the murderer. He had admitted the act; he had done it over his own signature. He had frankly avowed that it was a political homicide, for political ends, and to change the administration. Very naturally, there was a deep feeling of alarm, as usual in such a case, lest he might not be alone in the crime. Political revolutions are rarely wrought through assassination, except in confederacy, as a result of conspiracy. Recently one of the crowned heads of Europe had been openly assassinated in the presence of his troops and the great officers of the empire. It was found, that there was a communistic, socialistic, or nihilistic organization, in confederacy with the assassin. In repeated instances the same thing had happened in other countries. It had happened in our own country in a memorable case, after the close of the civil war, and there too it was found that confederates were parties to the crime. Entertaining these apprehensions, the then Attorney-General sent the chief of the detective service to the prisoner at midnight. That morning the President was alive and well; that night he was lying prostrate, speechless, helpless, and mortally wounded. The detective entered the cell. This gentlemanly, and moral, and Christian, and praying prisoner remonstrated against the intrusion upon so distinguished a person as Mr. Charles Julius Guiteau, to interrogate him about so trivial a matter as the murder of the President a few hours before. He, however, condescended in the end to answer the questions. You have heard the testimony of Mr. Brooks. Guiteau avowed the act and his motive; he stated it was purely political and patriotic. The witness says, at page 1728, that Guiteau told him, "He was lying in wait for him one night near the White House; that the President came out, and *his first impulse was to kill him then*. The President was alone and he could have done it, but somehow he was restrained from doing it." *He did not allege that God had commanded it. He made no pretense of inspiration.* He claimed that he shot him "from patriotic motives to unify the party." The Attorney-General went further. It turned out in the investigation that Guiteau had resided in Chicago; that he had studied law with General Reynolds, an eminent member of the Illinois bar, a gentleman whose brother had been appointed to an office under the government. A telegram was sent asking him to come to Washington, as it was supposed that he would be more likely than another, to ascertain whether there was in fact any socialistic or communistic plot at the bottom of the homicide. General Reynolds came. He saw the Attorney-General, Mr. Secretary Lincoln, and Mr. Secretary Kirkwood, members of the Cabinet. They gave him their instructions. He conferred also with Colonel Corkhill, and obtained permission from him to visit the jail. He did so, and heard the statements of the prisoner on two successive days. He reduced them to writing. He made notes in the presence of the prisoner, who had long known him. He did not tell him his object, further than that he was stimulated by curiosity, and that it was by the government's permission that he came. It is said, by counsel, that he did not deal frankly with the prisoner; that he was a spy, and that he was attempting to deceive the prisoner. He was first charged with falsehood, but that was retracted. All that he said in relating the conversations the prisoner has himself confirmed from the dock. He complains, however, that General Reynolds did not treat him like *a gentleman.*

The PRISO ER. I did not say it was all true. *I said it was generally true.*

Mr. PORTER. The material fact as to the conversation is, that *it was* generally true. But there are two other very material facts. One is that on the 18th of July, immediately after the first conversation, Guiteau wrote an address to the American people, which is here now in his own handwriting, and which is absolutely fatal to his present defense. Another important fact is, that on the following day, after reflecting upon the line of defense to which he should resort, he wrote a letter, in which he, for the first time, hints the word " inspiration," and even then *forgets* that he killed General Garfield by *God's command.* That paper is before you. Every letter and syllable is written by the hand of Charles J. Guiteau, and over his signature. That letter is equally fatal. They both prove the falsehood of his defense of supposed inspiration. They both prove his actual motive. They both point unmistakably to cold-blooded, deliberate, and well-planned murder. What Colonel Corkhill has done, has been to prove these facts, after he had ascertained them. It so happened that the original papers were returned to Attorney-General MacVeagh. When counsel for the government first conferred together, those papers were not before us, and we did not know what were their contents, nor what had become of them. They could not be found at the department, and it was not until the trial was far advanced, that we were enabled to trace them through the aid of General Reynolds. It happened that in the confusion of leaving Washington, they had been intermingled with a large number of other papers which had not yet been assorted. They were afterwards brought here, produced, and verified. If those papers had not been forthcoming, there might have been the chance of a dissenting juror, involving the necessity of another trial. But providentially they are here, and are in evidence. In the face of those papers, I shall show that they cannot ask any member of this jury to dissent from a verdict of guilty, without asking him to be untrue to his oath.

The PRISONER. I am very glad those papers are here. Attorney-General MacVeagh wouldn't have anything to do with the case.

Mr. PORTER. The prisoner evidently hopes to-day, that some member of the jury will, in the face of those documents, say that he was insane, and believe that he was commanded by God to do this murder.

It is claimed by the prisoner that the United States attorney is prosecuting him for the sake of inordinate fees. The counsel for the defense, who permit him to make these imputations, must know that the compensation of that officer is fixed by statute. He cannot draw one dollar from the United States Treasury, except as authorized by law, either for himself or for anybody else. With the concurrence of the Attorney-General he can do so for certain purposes, and upon proper vouchers. His pay is fixed by law. What do you suppose, gentlemen, is the enormous sum that has tempted Colonel Corkhill to enter into this alleged conspiracy? *Your* pay is meager enough. These two months and a half of your lives that you have been imprisoned for another's wrong, entitle you only to a mere pittance, and yet the pay of each of you is much larger than his. The law fixes his salary at two hundred dollars a year, with fees in each case, also regulated by law. What do you suppose to be his fee for the two months and a half that he has devoted to this trial? It is exactly twenty dollars. He has that sum for the trial of each case, and that is what he receives for this entire trial. If he had consulted his personal interests, his honor will tell you that it would have been, to have the trial completed in a day, or rather not to have had the case tried at all. Within these two months and a half, in the ordinary course of things, he might have had fifty trials disposed of, each bringing him twenty dollars. A great portion of our criminal trials are such as can be disposed of in a single day, each entitling the United States attorney to the same fee as in a case for the murder of the President. That is the position of Colonel Corkhill on this trial.

Now, with regard to my friend, Mr. Davidge? His fee has never been received, nor one dollar of it. It has never been liquidated or proposed to be liquidated. He has no existing claim against the government, and could not sue it under any circumstances. To meet these unfounded and reiterated assertions, which were made with a manifest and evil purpose, it is sufficient to explain to you the law. The government is supposed to be good and responsible. When there is occasion, the Attorney-General is authorized by law, to appoint special attorneys to aid in the prosecution of particular causes or classes of causes. That power was in this case acted on by him, with the concurrence and approval of the President and the Cabinet. It was exercised, by the designation of my friend, Mr. Davidge, who is a resident of the District of Columbia, and of myself, residing in the City of New York, to aid the United States attorney in conducting the proceedings against this prisoner. We were told, in the communication addressed to us by the Attorney-General, that it was by direction of the President and the Cabinet. We accepted the appointment. By law there is a provision, in accordance with which, when we received our commissions, it was provided that the compensation we should receive, should be fixed by the head of the judicial department of the government. No sum was proposed, no designated fee, either absolute or contingent ; but simply a provision that for the services which we should render, without reference to the result of the trial, we should receive such compensation as the Attorney-General for the time being, whenever the case should be tried, should fix as the fair value of our services. We can ask no more. He can grant no less. It rests simply in his judgment and sense of right whether we shall be paid anything or nothing.

It so happened that I never, so far as I am aware, met the then Attorney-General. In the meantime, he has retired from office. It so happens, unfortunately for me, that I never met, even to exchange salutations, the present eminent Attorney-General of the United States. I know them both well by reputation. I know the present incumbent of that high office by having heard, as one of a large audience, and on a memorable occasion, an address delivered in the park grounds in the City of New York, such as few have heard from a living man. It was no political address. It was a just and generous tribute to a dead statesman, whose name has been illustrious in our public history; a name connected with revolutionary memories and with the highest national honors. It was on the occasion of the unveiling of the statue erected to Alexander Hamilton by his son. On that occasion, it so happened that I saw, for the first time, the present Attorney-General, and it was refreshing to hear one statesman speak of another, in terms which lifted statesmanship as far above mere politics as the canopy of Heaven is above the earth which it spans. I refer to the incident in no other spirit than this: To remind you that it may by possibility be, that one, not when we were employed, Attorney-General of the United States, though he had held that high distinction in the State of Pennsylvania, may be something more than a scheming politician; that he may not be open to the vile and unworthy imputations cast by the defense upon all connected with the government; that he may not be ready to bargain with counsel for contingent fees, or to purchase witnesses, even if he had the funds wherewith to buy them, which the court will tell you he has not.

Gentlemen, our compensation will be assessed by an officer who is so upright, so independent and of such clear integrity, that nothing I could say would prevent him from doing justice to us, or induce him to do injustice to the government. If it should so happen, that in his estimation, on a review of this trial, our services are worth no more than the prisoner has assessed them at, he certainly will not give more nor even as much as the law gives to Colonel Corkhill. If we have been unfaithful to our trust, if we have entered, as the prisoner and his counsel allege, into a conspiracy to convict the accused of a crime of which we know him to be innocent, most certainly, in that event, I should regard the assessment of their value at twenty dollars as an over assessment by precisely that amount.

The Prisoner. That would be a large amount for you.

Mr. Porter. That is the estimation of the prisoner; but certainly the Attorney-General will give neither more nor less to Mr. Davidge and to me, whether you acquit or convict. It will be a simple question with him what the services are worth, and certainly if the prisoner and his counsel can so manage it this trial will not be brought to a conclusion until another Attorney-General shall, in the ordinary course of human affairs, become the successor of the present distinguished incumbent. So much for the relations of the counsel, who are arraigned as parties to this alleged criminal conspiracy to enforce the law by securing the conviction of a murderer. Gentlemen, I should say one thing more in this connection: Counsel perfectly understood the importance of inducing you to distrust the witnesses who were summoned in behalf of the government. For some two months the clamorous charge has come from the prisoner, who moves as a convenient puppet, and says the things which Mr. Scoville, his brother-in-law, afterwards repeats on his authority, that our witnesses were offered, or bargained for extraordinary sums, and were brought here for the purpose of convicting "this poor half imbecile," this gentlemanly, Christian, moral, prayer-making man, this murderer in the three-fold character of a lawyer, a politician and a theologian. Gentlemen, this is sheer fabrication. Not one witness, expert or otherwise, who has been summoned by us on this trial, whether by telegram or by subpœna, has received or bargained for one penny more than the mileage from the place whence he came, and the one dollar and twenty-five cents a day during his attendance in Washington. The *experts*, who have testified on both sides, have been paid by the government the precise fees received by other witnesses. It seems that one of them on our side and two of them on the other, erroneously supposed they were entitled to something more. The law does not give it to them, and they cannot claim it. Their expectations were founded on a very natural mistake. They knew that in the States generally, when experts are summoned, they are paid by the State government the usual fees which they would receive from private parties. Their attendance involves time, labor, investigation, absence from business, suspension of their ordinary sources of income, and expenses, as to which, of course, they are not indemnified by the small pay which the government allows. They were mistaken; they are entitled to no more under the law, and no man among them has been promised anything more, than the pay of an ordinary witness. Take for instance Dr. Gray, a gentleman who has two professorships, and who was summoned, not by his own procurement, but against his will. He was called here to make an examination, to ascertain whether this man was sane or insane. He was detained for two months and a half, paying his own expenses, which would not be expected of him in the case of ordinary parties. He swears that he was not summoned to testify *for the government;* but for the purpose of making an examination and reporting whether the prisoner was sane or insane. No human being suggested that his testimony should be paid for. His attendance entitled him by law to mileage from his home, and one dollar and twenty-five cents a day for each day he was detained here. In order that you may appreciate the injustice of the imputation, you will remember that not one word was ever said to him by any one about compensation. He came here at the instance of the United States attorney, and simply because, without any knowledge of his views, we thought him the best and most experienced expert in the United States. We knew his professional eminence; that he had been in personal charge of over 12,000 lunatics; and that he had been most signally successful. He was a man honored at home and abroad for his high character and distinguished learning and attainments. Are we subject to just reproach for summoning such a man to Washington to examine the prisoner, and report the result? He came, and made a full, fair, and careful examination. There was no concealment; there was no disguise. Dr. Gray told the prisoner who he was. He said to him frankly, that he visited him at the instance of the government, but it was for the purpose of finding out, by personal examination, whether he was sane or insane; that he need not answer any question he did not desire; that after he had given his answers, he would reduce them to writing and read them to him, and make any corrections the prisoner might propose. The prisoner, as you remember, confirms this statement, and says that Dr. Gray reported truly all that transpired in his cell. The result was that Dr. Gray came to the clear conclusion that the man was perfectly sane.

Now let us see how munificently he is rewarded, for what they call this *purchased* opinion. You will remember that he was here from a few days before the trial down to the close of the evidence, a period of more than two months, and the vouchers on file show the amount he received, $175.20. Do you suppose this can cover his fare both ways, and his expenses here. He has come and he has gone, when liberated from the discharge of his public duty. He has told you what he believed, from his extended experience in charge of the New York State Lunatic Asylum, his observation of the insane for over thirty years, and his personal examination of the prisoner, that he was sane beyond all question.

Dr. Worcester and several others of the experts were summoned in behalf of the prisoner by his counsel, who learned from published interviews with them, that they were of opinion, from what they had read in the newspapers, that he was insane. They frankly admitted, when sworn, that they had come to Washington with those opinions. You remember their occupying seats assigned to the experts for the prisoner. They observed him from day to day in court. They went to the jail and examined him there. They saw how different the man was when in jail, from what he was in court, where he was on dress parade. I believe there were eight of them in all, and they came to the conclusion that the man was sane and responsible. Counsel for the defendant were notified by them that this was their conclusion. They wished to be discharged. It would not do, however, after such a display, to dismiss them without a form of examination, and the ingenious gentlemen on the other side devised a hypothetical question; whether, assuming a state of facts, unsupported by the evidence, they would then consider him insane? You remember that though not in form, it was in effect, a question whether, if a man had a hereditary taint of insanity, exhibited insanity in his youth, exhibited it in his manhood, and at a subsequent date, being under the insane delusion that he was authorized and commanded by God to kill the President, proceeded, without cause, to kill him, such a man was sane or insane? Such a question answers itself. If a man is insane, he is of course insane. There they chose to leave it; not to one of these eight experts did they venture to put the question, whether, *from their examination and observation of the prisoner*, they believed him to be insane. Not to one of their witnesses, except Dr. Spitzka, was any such question addressed. Is not the omission significant and suggestive? We asked those of their experts, who could do so without inconvenience, to remain, and they testified, as our experts did, that *on personal examination they found the prisoner sane.* Under those circumstances, gentlemen, I hope you will not believe that the experts whom Mr. Scoville has selected as fit subject for indictment, as conspirators against the prisoner, really have been guilty of selling themselves for money to the government, especially as the counsel and the prisoner do not agree, one of them fixing their imaginary price at $100 a day, and the other at $200 a day, without a scintilla of evidence in support of either assertion.

You appreciate the difficulty, gentlemen, of replying to counsel, with a lack not only of prearranged order and method, but of ordinary physical strength. For over nine days you have been addressed by three counsel for the defense, in the opening and concluding arguments. Of course, upon the evidence, they could not hope for a verdict of acquittal. Such a verdict would shock all christendom.

The PRISONER. (Interjecting.) A conviction would shock the public.

Mr. PORTER. The whole struggle has evidently been to persuade some one man out of the twelve, the apostolic number, to be untrue to his trust. Who it is, they hope to mislead, I do not know. Mr. Reed made it very evident that he thought there would be one, or, perhaps more, and Mr. Scoville, I think, indicated his concurrence in such an expectation. Such hopes usually rest on idle conjecture, and sometimes find support in still more idle rumors. Each of you has been examined on oath, and both sides have accepted you as fair and impartial jurymen. We have heard of nothing in the antecedents of either of your number, which would lead us to doubt his purpose to find a verdict according to the evidence. But we cannot fail to see, that the last seven days of argument has been mainly addressed to the single point of procuring a division of this jury. Such a result, under the circumstances of this case, would be very unfortunate.

Here is a confessed homicide, who establishes his guilt by his own oath. Is there a juror here, who will say upon his oath, that the prisoner is not guilty! The prisoner calls his act an "*assassination*," over his own signature. Can a juror find that it was "no assassination?" Would there not be a strange discordance between the proof and the response? What a dialogue :

PRISONER. Murder.
JUROR. No Murder.
PRISONER. Sane.
JUROR. Insane.

Gentlemen, the only consequence of a disagreement by you, upon such evidence, would be to call the attention not only of this country but of mankind to the fact, that a human being could, under such circumstances, think it his duty to shield the assassin of the President. But what would be accomplished by a disagreement? Is it supposed that the government of this country is not strong enough to press the case to a conclusion? A disagreement would defeat the purposes of this particular trial, and it might compel other jurors in due time to succeed you in your labors, to become prisoners in their turn, as you have been, as the consequence of another's crime, to be secluded, as you have been, from their families and business, and to have so much cut out of their lives, simply because, when the prisoner's evidence establishes his sanity and guilt a juror declines so to find.

The theory of the defense, as presented by Mr. Scoville, was plausible, but unfounded and illusory. He chose to embark his client's fortunes in a bark, which the prisoner with his own hand has scuttled. The case is brought down by him to the single question, whether on the 2d day of July, 1881, the assassin believed that he was commanded by God to murder the President.

The PRISONER. (Interjecting.) That is all there is to it, and that is what that jury will pass upon.

Mr. PORTER. (Continuing.) You perceive that the prisoner agrees with me. He saw it clearly from the beginning of the trial. If his counsel had the clear intelligence of the prisoner, they would have also seen it, and concentrated their strength upon that single issue.

Gentlemen, let me suggest to you, in reply to the remarks on your province, that a juror's oath is not an idle form, nor is his an irresponsible trust. I do not remember who it was that first suggested, what has often been repeated, "that under the various forms of government, of Anglo-Saxon origin, the ultimate security of all rights, all liberties, all protection is to be found in the jury box." In yonder Capitol, *districts* are represented in the House, *States* in the Senate, but in neither the body of the American people. There are under our form of government two potential representatives of *the people*. The one is the head of the nation—the President of the United States; the other is found in the jury, to which, in the last resort, our most essential rights, whether of life, liberty, or property, come for enforcement and protectection. For this purpose, under the operation of our laws, you are here to-day representing *the American people*, of whom the prisoner talks so clamorously. I do not mean, of course, that you represent them in any other sense, than as clothed with their authority, selected from their number, and bound to respect and enforce the laws they have ordained, to maintain the rights they have declared, and observe the obligations they have imposed. It is true that you are not to be influenced in any degree by popular opinion, whether it be or be not in harmony with the dictates of your own judgments and consciences. It sometimes happens, however, that issues arise involving great questions of right and wrong, on which all honest and right-minded men are substantially agreed. It seems to us that this is one of those cases. The homicide arrested universal attention, because it was a brazen and bloody act ; not committed in the secrecy of night, but under the broad canopy of Heaven, in the open light of day ; because it was committed, not merely against the murdered victim, but in full view of his private relations, family relations, State relations, public relations, affecting the welfare and stability of the government itself ; so far, at least, as a change of political administration was sought to be affected by lawless violence. In such a case, it is not to be expected that jurors should regard the act with less loathing and abhorrence than other men. Aware of this, the prisoner has been clamorously assuring you from day to day, *that the people of this country were now all on his side ;* that he was constantly receiving letters of approval, and large pecuniary contributions, and that the newspapers, from which you are excluded, but which he professed to be reading, holding them ostentatiously before him while he was watching the progress of the trial, were all declaring themselves in his favor. You may well have wondered how it was, that, while he was making these constant allegations, his counsel did not second his appeals to the public opinion, either of the city of Washington, of the District of Columbia, of the United States, or of mankind. I confess I have yet to see the first newspaper, published in this country, that ventures to defend the action of this prisoner. I have seen occasional articles before the trial began, and some since, questioning whether he was not insane, but many more, and as I think very unjustly, censuring the court, and the administration of justice, because he was not already tried and convicted.

Mr. SCOVILLE. Does the Court allow that kind of talk to the jury?

Mr. PORTER. I cannot permit these statements of the prisoner to pass without contradiction. I have been censured recently in numerous letters for allowing these statements before the jury to be uncontradicted.

Mr. SCOVILLE. I want to know if Judge Porter is arguing to the jury or the Court, that is all. If he is going to testify now, I propose to give the same sort of testimony—I propose to give my letters.

Mr. PORTER. The gentleman is mistaken. He has already given his testimony. And you must bear in mind that Mr. Reed and Mr. Scoville have both occupied much of your time within the last six of the seven days, in deprecating your being influenced by public opinion, or the outside sentiment of the country, and claiming that you or some of your number should refuse to find a verdict of conviction, on the ground that otherwise a poor lunatic was being hurried on to the gallows.

Mr. SCOVILLE. If the Court please, Judge Porter is not permitted to give any sort of evidence at this stage of the case. If he is allowed to take that course I shall insist upon the same thing.

The COURT. I understand that Judge Porter's remarks are in reply to the prisoner's statement. To that extent I think it is admissible and not beyond that.

Mr. PORTER. Now, gentlemen——

Mr. SCOVILLE. One moment, one moment; I want to settle this question now. Now, if Judge Porter had made this statement in any other way, by putting him upon the stand to correct him, or anything of that kind, then it would have been proper. Now, if the prisoner made a statement here while the case was in progress of trial he had the opportunity to put him on the stand under oath and ask him to produce these letters. We have now got to a stage of the case where we are arguing before the jury, and Judge Porter is producing what is equivalent to his deposition here in this case as evidence, as matter of fact. Now, I say if that is to be permitted to go on here for five minutes it can go on for an hour, and Judge Porter can occupy days with these statements that have no foundation in fact, that are not before the Court as matter of evidence at all, and yet work them in just as sworn statements before the jury.

The COURT. No, I do not think he can go further than to simply contradict the prisoner's assertion that he was receiving commendations from the public and newspapers—to contradict that line of statements which the prisoner has constantly been giving to them.

Mr. PORTER. Gentlemen, I call your attention to the fact that while the prisoner himself has been endeavoring to convince you that the public was on his side——he——

Mr. SCOVILLE. I propose to take an exception to these statements now made with the permission of the court to this jury, and I wish the record to show that I have duly objected to the statements, and that the court permitting him to make them in the form and manner in which he has made them is excepted to.

Mr. PORTER. I have made statements so far which have not been excepted to. I propose to go on and make another for the purpose of showing that *I am right*, and that you have acknowledged it.

Mr. SCOVILLE. Now then; I except now. I wish the exception to be noted on the record to the permission of these statements of Judge Porter to go to that jury.

The COURT. What statements?

Mr. SCOVILLE. The statements which he has made now, and which the record for the last three minutes shows probably as to what the public sentiment is as to what newspapers state as to his proving letters. I object to every one of those statements going to the jury, and ask to have them ruled out.

The COURT. I do not sanction any statement about letters received by him, statements of newspapers, or anything else except simply to contradict the prisoner's repeated statements.

Mr. PORTER. Gentlemen, I wish to call your attention to the argument of the counsel. If it were true, as the prisoner has alleged, that the American press are on his side, that the leading journals are on his side, why was it that his counsel, when they came to sum up to you, did not follow his lead, but insisted that you should not be influenced by public opinion?

Mr. SCOVILLE. If the Court please, I insist upon a suspension of Judge Porter's remarks, so that I can get my exception ruled upon. Now, if the Court please, I understood your honor to say that you sustained Judge Porter in saying precisely what he has now said to that jury upon this ground: That the prisoner during the trial made statements substantially of the same character as to the opinions of the press and as to correspondence received by him, and that now, when Judge Porter, in his address to the jury, states those things as facts which he says are true as to the current literature of the newspapers as to what they say upon this subject, as to private letters, when your honor permits those things to go to the jury and I attempt to call the gentleman to order and your honor still permits him to go on with those statements, that is what I desire to object to and take an exception upon.

The COURT. I have not given permission that those statements should go on at all. The statements were made before the exception was fully stated.

Mr. SCOVILLE. I have tried to talk at the same time with the gentleman, but I have not been able to get a word in.

The COURT. I know; but both counsel were talking at once, and I have been unable to hear your full statement.

Mr. PORTER. (To Mr. Scoville.) If you have any request to make, your request should be made to the Court.

The DISTRICT ATTORNEY. Let me say one word. The prisoner, appearing as counsel for himself, is allowed not only to state what the public sentiment was, but he was allowed——

Mr. SCOVILLE. He was not allowed to do anything of the sort, but he did it without being allowed.

The DISTRICT ATTORNEY. Yes; but he appeared as counsel for himself, and in his address to the jury he read extracts from the *New York Herald*, he read editorials, and he stated to the jury what public sentiment was, and he read private letters. Judge Porter's remarks were merely contradictory to that, and the gentleman has no right to interrupt him or take exceptions to it.

Mr. SCOVILLE. The gentlemen ought to have objected. If they did not object to what the prisoner did, I object to what Judge Porter is doing.

The COURT. I know the prisoner said what was objectionable, but it could not be prevented.

Mr. SCOVILLE. Cannot Judge Porter be prevented?

The COURT. I think Judge Porter ought not to refer to the newspapers or to what his letters contain on the subject.

Mr. PORTER. When he refers to them with a positive statement, can I not deny it?

The COURT. Undoubtedly you can deny positive statements, but any statement as to what the newspapers contain or as to letters is not allowed on either side.

Mr. SCOVILLE. I desire the record to show my exception.

Mr. PORTER. (Addressing the jury.) I will read what this man said at page 1749—

You ought to be ashamed of yourself—

addressing my associate, Mr. Davidge—

God Almighty will curse you prosecuting men for the mean, dirty way in which you have done your work. *That is the unanimous opinion of the American press to-day.*

The PRISONER. That is a very light statement. I gave the jury a specimen of public sentiment in my speech. *That Philadelphia letter shows* the case well.

Mr. PORTER. Here is a telegram which was read to you by him, and which appears at page 1572. It was read by this prisoner in open Court, not as a witness, but as counsel for himself:

The PRISONER. Some of the leading people of America consider me a very fine fellow. Last night at 8 o'clock I received the following telegram from Boston for the edification of this court and jury and the American people: (Reading.)

" Mr. CHARLES J. GUITEAU, *Washington, D. C.*
" Old Boston——

The PRISONER. (Correcting the reading.) " All Boston."

Mr. PORTER. (Continuing to read)—

"sympathizes with you. You are yet to be President.
"A HOST OF ADMIRERS."

I don't know but two men in America who want me hung; one is Judge Porter, because he expects to get $5,000; the other is Mr. Corkhill. Corkhill is booked to be removed anyway, and he wants to get even with me, because he thinks I am the man that did it. It is said I am too severe in my language. I want to say a word about that: "Woe unto you, ye hypocrites, scribes and Pharisees! How can ye escape damnation in hell? Ye generation of vipers! how can ye escape the damnation of hell?" Who said that? Who uses that language? The meek and lowly Jesus, the meek and lowly Jesus. I put my ideas in sharp language, and I have the example of the Saviour of mankind for doing it. He called things by their right names. *When any one assaulted Him He struck back. He didn't lay down like a craven, nor I don't.*

The PRISONER. Correct.

Mr. PORTER. I did not intend to refer to that particular passage at this point, but I will. These are some of his representations, first, as to public sentiment; second, as to the opinion of the press; and, third, as to the Redeemer of mankind. It is true that the Second Person of the Trinity, when for our redemption He assumed our form and made Himself our brother, did speak on topics which were appropriate to this case. I refer to the dialogue between the scribes and Pharisees—the men who made long prayers and who wore broad phylacteries—the canters of those days —when they fell into dialogue with the Saviour, and put forth their dispensation as this man now puts forth his. I read from viii. John, 39th verse:

They answered and said unto Him, Abraham is our father—

They belonged to the Abrahamic school of which the prisoner has said so much—

Jesus said unto them, if ye were Abraham's children, ye would do the works of Abraham.

Abraham did not go to the grave with his hands reddened in the blood of murder. Again, at verse 43:

Why do ye not understand my speech? *Even* because ye cannot hear my word—

But this disciple of the Abrahamic school claimed that *he* did. Let us see how they were dealt with—

Ye are of *your father the devil*, and the lusts of your father ye will do. He was a murderer from the beginning, and abode not in the truth, because there is no truth in him. When he speaketh a lie, he speaketh of his own, for he is a liar, and the father of it.

(Argument suspended.)

The COURT. We will adjourn the Court until to-morrow morning.

Thereupon (at 1 o'clock and five minutes) the Court was adjourned until to-morrow morning at 10 o'clock.

TUESDAY, *January* 24, 1882.

The Court met at 10 o'clock; counsel for Government and accused being present.

Mr. PORTER. If it please your honor—

The PRISONER. (Interrupting.) I desire to say, before Judge Porter proceeds, that some crank has signed my name to a letter in the papers this morning. I repudiate that kind of business. I also understand that two cranks have been arrested this morning. One or two of them have been laying around here since Saturday. I wish to say that I am in charge of this Court and its officers, and if any one attempts to do me harm, *they will be shot dead on the spot.* Understand that. When I get outside I can take care of myself.

Mr. PORTER. (Continuing.) Gentlemen of the jury: As usual the Court has been opened by the prisoner, but by his permission I am at liberty to add a few words. I am grateful to you for the indulgence which has enabled me to proceed this morning. If I had done so yesterday, in the present condition of my health, my strength would have been utterly exhausted. But, if able, I shall continue, and to the end. It may be needful, for aught I know, to trespass still farther on your indulgence, and yet I feel that you who are engaged, as we are, in this thankless and weary task, you who have endured patiently during this long period, longer even than the fast of forty days in the wilderness, in an atmosphere dark and putrid with calumny and blasphemy, will extend some indulgence to those who speak in behalf of the Government and the law.

I endeavored yesterday to show you that this defense was one founded on sham, pretense, and imposture; on brazen falsehood; which was supposed to acquire force and strength by perpetual reiteration. The disciples of the school of Guiteau have great confidence in a maxim of Aaron Burr, which, with a slight deviation from its original form, would apply with singular pertinence to this defense: "Truth is that which is uttered with effrontery, enforced by persistency, and embedded by reiteration." There are set phrases of the counsel which have rung like bell peals through the whole trial, sometimes discordant with each other and with the mock inspirations of Guiteau; but whether with each other, or with the blatant and turbulent utterances of the prisoner, all clashing with the honest truth of the case; the truth which you are to assert and declare.

I endeavored to show you, that Guiteau had falsified by his persistent acts his mock and empty professions; that he had belied by his life the character claimed for him by the opening counsel; that this prayerful, moral and Christian man, as he was fancifully pictured to you, was, in fact, a liar, a swindler, and a murderer at heart, from the beginning—

not acting by special Divine appointment—for it so happens, that under our dispensation depravity does not develop itself, in a legal sense, until one has reached the age, when he is presumed to know the distinction between right and wrong—that he has grown worse every year that he has lived, since he attained that age; that he was a vicious and a disobedient child; that he was lawless and ungrateful to his father; that he was an unfilial brother; that he stung every man who was his benefactor, from his youth up; that he had an intense desire for public notoriety, and that this manifested itself, even as early as when he was seventeen years of age; that his vanity was inordinate, and that his spirit of selfishness, jealousy, and hate overleaped all bounds and restraints. All these things we know of him, even in his early life. I shall call your attention to some of the evidences of these substantially undisputed facts; showing that he continued growing worse and worse, until his career culminated in a cold-blooded and cruel assassination. It was consistent and harmonious with the vicious propensities he had betrayed from the beginning. There is a self propagating property in sin, and vice, and crime, by which it is constantly swelling and enlarging itself, until it thoroughly intones the whole nature of the man, and shapes him—not *by birth* as Dr. Spitzka would have you believe, but *by assiduous culture*—into "a moral montrosity." Gentlemen, the same man who, through his counsel, in effect and substance, asked you, his counsel being unsworn, and knowing that you were sworn, to overlook the obligations of your oaths—that same man presumed to arraign the counsel for the government as conspirators, coolly confederating against this innocent Christian agent of God, to hang him for a confessed homicide. And what was the grave imputation, aside from that which I referred to yesterday, of our being bought by somebody—he did not say whom, and for specific sums—which the leading counsel averred and changed from time to time to suit the varying exigencies of the cause; aside from the charge that we, who had never received a penny ourselves, and were not bound or authorized to pledge the faith of the government to others under any circumstances, had suborned witnesses to perjury. Aside from this, I wish to call your attention now to another ground of accusation, which is resorted to, not needlessly, for they needed all that has been done for the prisoner and more, but which, it is evident, they thought needful, to induce in you a belief that the government had deliberately suppressed evidence which we were bound to offer, and which forsooth the two Guiteaus expected from us as matter of right in their behalf.

Gentlemen, what is the nature of the evidence which is said to have been suppressed? The prisoner's counsel claim, that we were bound to establish his sham defense, and to do it by his unsworn declarations in his own behalf. This is the effect and substance of their argument. In other words, we were bound to set up in his behalf a false defense, and to aid it by proving any and all unsworn declarations of the prisoner. It seems that the government, in the exercise of the power, which is uniformly acted on by every State and every national government, for the purpose of detecting and bringing to justice all implicated in a public crime, sent those to the cell of the prisoner, who were charged with the public duty of ascertaining and reporting the facts, not to the court, but to the government, for the purpose of controlling and determining its action. The effect of the report which was made, of this man's statements of the history of his life, and the circumstances connected with the homicide, is shown by the practical result. The government ordered his prosecution for the crime. That government consists of those, whom he now coolly and impudently claims as his pretended beneficiaries. The whole office of the statement which he made to Mr. Bailey, the stenographer of the United States attorney, so far as the government was concerned, was to ascertain whether he had any accomplices in the crime. It was taken as it fell from the lips of the culprit, to the end that the government should know whether there was any excuse or palliation for the homicide, and whether any others than the immediate actor were involved in its perpetration.

The PRISONER. Mr. MacVeagh would not prosecute after he got Brook's report.

Mr. PORTER. As Mr. Attorney-General MacVeagh was the government officer who communicated to me, not only his own direction for the prosecution, but the concurring authority of the President and the Cabinet, I leave it for you to say, whether you credit the impudent assertion of the prisoner, that any one connected with the government has, at any time, been ready to dip his hands in the President's blood or to shelter his assassin. The counsel for the prosecution have been at all times subject to the order of the government. If I were to receive to-day from the Executive, or from Attorney General Brewster, a direction to suspend this prosecution, my argument would close the instant the communication reached my hand. I should be from that moment, as mute as the dead President. These shams and impostures will not serve the prisoner's purpose. He might, as well attempt to escape from the jaws of a closing vise, as from the overwhelming force of the testimony by such railing accusations. Mr. Scoville is a gentleman of sufficient intelligence to know, that the record made for the information of the government did not belong to him, and could not be called for by him, that it was not at his disposal, any more than what passed in the private consultations between the United States attorney and his clerk, any more than the confidential communications between counsel and client, any more than private and personal communications between physician and patient; yet you, day after day, have been told that the government was *suppressing* testimony, which had been furnished by the statements of Guiteau, in his own behalf, to a stenographer.

The declarations of this man, as he claims, were intended by him to appear in the New York *Herald.* No matter for whom they were dictated; *they were nothing but his unsworn declarations;* and nobody, except the Government, could introduce them, for the purpose of proving the facts he alleged. On the *side issue of insanity,* his honor very properly permitted him to prove, as far as he could, *his own declarations, no matter whether true or false,* for the purpose of showing, not *the truth* of the alleged facts, but the then state of his mind. But he could not demand from the counsel for the Government, the production of his unsworn statements, which, if we had offered them, would have made them evidence. You have been told in substance by Mr. Scoville, again and again, that the prisoner's statement, made and extended through the entire months of July and August, did allege that the killing was *by the command of God.* If we had introduced that statement of the prisoner, we should have made it evidence of every fact contained in it. Gentlemen, bear in mind, on this point, that I cannot speak, except in contradiction of the allegations of the prisoner and his counsel. I, who know what the paper is, deny that it contains any allegation of inspiration.

Mr. SCOVILLE. I object now, if the Court please. I hope I am in time to make my exception.

The COURT. Yes ; that is objectionable.

Mr. PORTER. Is it objectionable to deny the unproved allegation of the prisoner ?

The COURT. I think so.

Mr. PORTER. No, sir ; what he asserted was, that *it contains* the statement that it was commanded by God. Your honor does not know ; the jury does not know. I oppose my statement to his, and deny it.

The COURT. I do not think you ought to state anything that is either contained, or not contained in that statement.

Mr. PORTER. Then I am compelled to submit.

The COURT. Your first argument is very correct ; that you could not put that in evidence without putting in evidence the whole ; that it might contain a great many facts.

Mr. PORTER. No, sir ; but the point is here : You permit not only the prisoner, but his counsel, to aver that a paper *not in evidence* contains a a statement that the killing was by the command of God. That I deny.

The COURT. No ; I permitted his counsel simply to argue from its nonproduction, that the jury might infer it contained something prejudicial to the prosecution. But unless you take the stand as a witness I do not think you are at liberty to state what the paper contains or omits.

Mr. PORTER. (To the jury.) On the contrary, gentlemen, and I have practiced law longer than his honor, I beg to say, that where there is an unfounded assertion——

Mr. SCOVILLE. I insist upon stopping that gentleman making declarations in defense.

Mr. PORTER. Where a false assertion, unwarranted by the evidence, is made by either prisoner or counsel, we may contradict it.

The COURT. I cannot allow anything to be said about the *contents* of that paper.

Mr. PORTER. I have not stated anything about the contents, but I have denied what is affirmed as a fact by the prisoner, without proof.

The COURT. But if you deny that it contains certain things, I do not think that is proper.

Mr. PORTER. I say that it does not contain, what they allege, without proof, it does contain.

The COURT. I do not think you are at liberty to do that.

Mr. PORTER. As the government cannot except to your honor's ruling, I must submit; but I do not admit that the prisoner or his counsel can make a statement of fact unwarranted by the evidence, which I cannot contradict.

The COURT. The prisoner was on the stand as a witness.

Mr. PORTER. *He was in the dock*, and not on the stand. It was no part of his testimony. It was from there (indicating the dock).

The COURT. Of course that cannot go in.

Mr. PORTER. Mr. Scoville was not a witness; has not been sworn, and I shall presently come to the question, why not? But that would be anticipating.

Again, gentlemen, we are criticised as government conspirators—and one of the counts of the indictment is, that we put in *too much evidence*. We had no right, it is said, to call witness after witness to prove the circumstances attending the death of the President. We should have tried this cause in a day, or a week on our side, and left the prisoner full swing for the rest of the two months and a half; that we were not at liberty to call *all* the witnesses for it was enough that we proved *by one* the fact that Guiteau fired at the President.

Gentlemen, I think you will see that in the course of the argument, it has been made very evident, that we called only the right witnesses, and to the right points. But they tell you an indecent and outrageous thing was done. We brought into the court the flattened bullet that quenched the President's life.

The PRISONER. (Interjecting.) The doctors did that.

Mr. PORTER. So the prisoner says; and so he said at the beginning of the trial. It was claimed that this was not a murderous weapon, murderously aimed. Yet the bullet was driven home with such a crushing force, that you could not get either end of the ball, after it passed through the President's spine, to enter again the cartridge that had contained it. When it was driven into a shapeless form, by the act of the murderer and the resistance of the backbone of the murdered man, the production of the penetrated vertebra was, forsooth, an indecent thing in a court of justice. You know, of course, what a howling clamor would have been raised, by the prisoner and his counsel, if, after a post-mortem examination, we had failed to produce it. We were just as much bound to do it, in the case of the President, as of an ordinary citizen. We are told, that in a case, where *medical malpractice was one of the issues in the cause*, asserted constantly from the prisoner's box, it was discreditable that we should not leave the wound to description from memory, and that the path of the ball through the spine should not be traced by its own indelible marks, in order to falsify the prisoners's pretense that the doctors killed the President. It became necessary in the course of the post-mortem examination to detach that portion of the spine. It was, as it should be, preserved to be used upon the trial, so that the truth of the case should not be left to rest, on the uncertain, and, perhaps, conflicting memory of witnesses. The prisoner seems to have had a delicate and sacred regard for the particular portion of the President's backbone, through which the ball passed. He seems to have had less regard for it, when he drove that bullet through it. His grief, and that of his counsel, seems to be, that the shot left its track, so that the jury could see the direction of the ball, and the power of the chosen weapon of death, and the falsity of the pretense that the doctors killed him. This was a phase of the defense we were bound to anticipate, and we did precisely what would have been done in a like case in any court in Christendom. Yet this is charged as grave evidence of a government conspiracy against this innocent assassin.

Again, we have a daring and insolent attempt, after the learned judge, in pursuance of his duty, had settled and declared the law—an attempt made alike by the prisoner and his counsel—to question the authority of his rulings. It is our duty on that subject, to maintain the binding force of those rulings, and the clear authority of the Court to instruct the jury as to the law.

For the evident purpose of leading you to disregard the instructions already given to the jury, you are told by the prisoner's counsel that you are "kings and emperors;" that you are responsible to no one for your action; that you are at liberty to act on your own individual views, not only upon what *is* proved, but upon what is *not* proved; that you may assume the existence of facts in conflict with the evidence adduced, and base your verdict on possibilities and conjecture, unrestrained by legal rules. Gentlemen, it is the absolute province of the Court to declare the law. You are bound to render a verdict according to the evidence, and that upon the issues submitted to you by the Judge. You are to receive the law, not from the counsel, not from the prisoner, but from the Court. When, after the law has been definitely settled by the presiding judge, the defendant and his counsel take occasion to argue that the Court is wrong, and to demand that he should modify his charge, it is appropriate for me to refer for a single moment, to two decisions which contradict the assertions, on which their allegation is predicated; not as authority, for I deny that any authority is needed to settle the clear proposition, that the instructions the Judge has given to you are, for the purposes of this case, unquestioned law; but for the simple reason, that a Chief Justice of the Supreme Court of one of the leading States in the Union, has been insolently and summarily arraigned before you, as a party to an unworthy attempt to hang "this innocent lunatic"; and I therefore, without saying one word more in regard to it, call your honor's attention, if there should be occasion for you to advert to that censure upon a fellow-judge, to the fact, that so far from that Judge having declared the law, on this question of the responsibility of the insane, in violation of all previous law, your honor will feel at liberty to say that it was in accordance, with the reported decisions of five judges and ex-judges of the Supreme Court of the United States, and with the only reported decisions in the Federal tribunals, including what I regard as the concurring decision of the Supreme Court of the United States, in 98 United State Reports. In that connection, I invite your honor's attention to the case reported in the Washington Law Reporter, issued on the 18th of the present month, and which only reached us five days ago—concurrently with the counsel making his strangely unwarranted assertions, and the prisoner making his insolent allegations in regard to Chief Justice Davis—in the case of the State against Martin, in which Judge Depue charged the jury, in a case presented for judgment *before this trial commenced*, a New Jersey case, tried in the month of October last, in the very State in which General Garfield ceased to breathe, and where the prisoner says he would wish to have been tried—in which that learned Judge declares the law, in precise accordance with Mr. Davidge's unaltered requests, and in which he, in harmony with the views of the judges to whose decisions we referred on the argument, though not wholly with your honor's view, as I understand it, that the prisoner must overcome the legal presumption of sanity by a *clear preponderance of proof*. In that respect he went further than your honor, and further than Judge Davis; and I submit that it is not to be assumed by the jury, that one of the so-called wrongs of the prosecution is, that we cited a *nisi prius* decision by the Chief Justice of the Supreme Court of New York, as against the *nisi prius* citations of the prisoner.

Mr. REED. If the Court please, I desire to make a suggestion. Judge Porter, if you are to discuss questions of law over again, it is but fair to submit the authorities to us. I want to say now here that I repudiate and deny the statement of the gentleman that I have in any manner and at any time or in any place questioned the law——

Mr. PORTER. (Interrupting.) Did I say that you had?

Mr. REED. (Continuing.) As laid down by the Court. Now if there is to be new law introduced, and new discussion, we want the authorities, and we will answer them.

The COURT. Very well.

Mr. PORTER. It is only to be introduced *on the other side*, according to the theory of the gentlemen. I do not admit it to be within your honor's discretion, even on the appeal of counsel, to reverse your already announced decision. It is conclusive upon us, although it is not in full accordance with our views. Your honor, I know, understands why I say this. Mr. Reed is, in one sense, as the witness Amerling is, counsel for the defendant. But the leading counsel for the defendant sits behind him, in conjunction with the prisoner in the dock. They are the two responsible counsel for the defense.

In regard to the other decision, which has been repeatedly brought to the attention of your honor, although uniformly stated incorrectly; it happens that the case in the Court of Appeals, which is said to have adopted the new view of the law, according to the dispensation of Guiteau, and to be a great advance upon the antecedent law, which actually called on the prisoner to rise and thank the judges of the Court of Appeals in New York for coming over to his side——

The PRISONER. (Interjecting.) Exactly what they did.

Mr. PORTER. (Continuing.) I will hand their decision to your honor, if you should have occasion to refer to it in your charge. In the view I take of it, however, you will have no occasion to refer to it, because you will declare, not what their opinion of the law is, but what your own is. Still, as it happens that this decision comes from my own State, and from its highest tribunal, and is in precise accord with what I stated to your honor in the argument, to be the law of New York, and in precise accordance with which your honor framed your instructions in respect to the question of the *onus probandi*, and the effect of a reasonable doubt, I desire merely to call your attention to the decision; because the subject is not generally understood, and, as commonly conceded, the majority of the State Courts and the Federal tribunals have held otherwise. But your honor adopted, what I believe to be the true and sound rule of law. As counsel for the government, I was bound, as a matter of course, to present the authorities on both sides, which I did, and I stated this to your honor as the rule prevailing in my own State; and it was for you to determine, whether you would follow the Federal tribunals and the rulings of the majority of the States, in accordance with Mr. Davidge's proposition, or what I confess, with my antecedent views, seemed to me to be the right rule upon principle. But lest I should be misunderstood, as the prisoner took occasion to tell the jury from the box——

Mr. Scoville. Interrupting. Now, if the Court please, I object to Judge Porter's reading this law. If the discussion is to go on before your honor upon legal questions, let us have his authorities and let us have an opportunity to answer them. I am perfectly willing he should hand it to the Court or anything of that kind. But if he is going to make a legal argument here, and cite decisions as to what the law is we want to know so as to answer it.

Mr. Porter. I will hand the decision to your honor. That will answer my purpose. (Submitting pamphlet to the Court.)

Gentlemen, this case—which the prisoner would have you believe, decided that if he knew right from wrong, it did not follow at all that he was guilty of murder, but, on the contrary, that he was not ; for that is the substance of his proposition, as you will remember—lays down the rule of responsibility in accordance with the proposition of Mr. Davidge, and while I do not personally agree to the qualification which his honor has made, but from his standpoint very properly, for the purpose of excluding a possible misapprehension in reference to future cases, and to cases arising on a different state of facts—yet the rule announced to you by the Court was so well understood to be the law, that in the New York case, it was not even made the ground of exception by counsel, though the charge of the judge at *nisi prius* was stated in the report of the case. The prisoner's counsel, however, *did* object that the Judge refused to charge, that if there was a reasonable doubt of the prisoner's sanity they must acquit.

That question came clearly before the Court of Appeals of New York, and although *my printed report* may be less authoritative than the *oral statement of the prisoner*, the Judge after reading, what, at the request of the defendant's counsel, I have submitted to him, will be able to instruct you, if there is occasion for it, that those ill-advised judges unanimously held, that the question of reasonable doubt *on insanity* did not arise, and that the request to charge the jury " that if there was a reasonable doubt of his insanity " was denied and properly denied, and that the only rule to prevail in such a case was precisely that which your honor has already delivered from the bench ; that is to say : the burden of proof is upon the prisoner to establish his insanity, and that he is *not* entitled to a charge that upon a reasonable doubt on that subject the jury should acquit; but that if, upon the whole evidence, the jury have a reasonable doubt of the *prisoner's guilt* then he is entitled to the benefit of the doubt.

The Prisoner. (Interjecting.) You and the Court of Appeals do not agree.

Mr. Porter. The judge will determine that matter, if there is occasion to determine it at all.

But, gentlemen, I wish you now to bear in mind, that though from causes which neither we nor the Court could control, and from successive incidents and utterances from the criminal dock, we singularly enough have at times had this court room converted, at the will and choice of the mocking assassin of Garfield, into what has popularly been known as the arena of a circus clown and murderer.

The PRISONER. (Interjecting.) That is false.

MR. PORTER. I know the difficulty the learned Judge has had and felt from the beginning. The public, who have censured or assumed to censure him, did not know, as he did, and as you did, the practical difficulties of the situation. We have all felt that it was important that this should be *a final trial;* that there should be no shadow of doubt, that the prisoner had every conceivable right, and when he ascertained that this was our purpose, *he proceeded to exercise others which were not his.* I was upon the proposition, gentlemen, that this defense, as well on the part of the prisoner as his counsel, has been *a disingenous and sham defense.* You would naturally have supposed, that when you laid your hands upon the book of God, and pledged yourselves to try faithfully this issue between the United States and the man whom the grand jury presented to you as the murderer and assassin of President Garfield, the inquiry by you was simply, "*Is this man guilty?*" How has that inquiry ramified since? You are not a jury *of inquisition* to find out who killed Garfield. Human memory would scarcely recall the various and protean forms to which this inquiry has been shaped. There has been a persistant attempt to make you think you are really here *as a jury of inquisition* to find out who killed Garfield, and before you were even sworn as jurors the issue, there has been a constant effort to shift the issue. You are asked who killed President Garfield. That he is dead most men frankly admit. Who killed him?

The PRISONER. (Interjecting.) The doctors.

Mr. PORTER. "The doctors," responds the prisoner.

The PRISONER. (Interjecting.) That is what most people think about it.

Mr. PORTER. Has or has not the defense that the doctors killed him been abandoned?

The PRISONER. The Lord allowed the doctors to confirm my act. They were the immediate cause of his death.

Mr. PORTER. I am afraid the prisoner has not had the latest intelligence from heaven, for he admits *inspiration* came and went an hour before and after he murdered the President.

A gentleman was assigned, on the application of the prisoner, to assist him in the defense of this case, and assigned too by the Court. It was in the assertion of a judicial power, which was properly exercised. The gentleman selected, MR. LEIGH ROBINSON, was one of the ablest lawyers either in this District or elsewhere. He was an accomplished jurist; he was an honorable man; he was a lawyer in the highest sense of the term, and as blood sometimes, though not always, tells, he had the prestige in both branches of his family, of names illustrious in the annals both of American statesmanship and of the American bar. He appeared in the case ; he discharged his duties faithfully ; he acted in accordance with his convictions ; he fully justified and vindicated the selection made by his honor, for he was a thorough and intoned gentleman; he was a man of honor; he was a lawyer who could descend to nothing unworthy of him; and having served faithfully up to a point in the trial, beyond which the prisoner would permit him to serve no longer, driven by ignominous insolence and abuse, and unmerited insult so far as this prisoner could offer personal indignity to a high-toned gentleman, and with still greater ignominy, so far as the senior counsel associated with him could offer it——

The PRISONER. (Interjecting.) That is false.

Mr. PORTER. (Continuing.)——Driven to ask his honor to relieve him from a position which it had become impossible for him, as an upright lawyer and an honorable gentleman to retain, your honor properly relieved him.

Let us ask now, *who killed Garfield?* The prisoner tells you, with his characteristic impudence and effrontery, that the responsibility is upon *Secretary Blaine.* Guiteau was *not*, but Blaine *was*, the murderer. Why I was led to think, from the prisoner's evidence, perhaps inadvertently, that the responsibility was on the Deity, who is beyond your jurisdiction. But the prisoner, who denied that he was the assassin, at page 692 of the evidence, puts forth the absurd and impudent pretense, that Secretary Blaine is responsible for the murder of President Garfield.

The PRISONER. (Interjecting.) *Morally* responsible.

Mr. PORTER. (Continuing.) Secretary Blaine, for whom, brilliant and eminent as he is, I have no more reason for particular regard than, so far as I know, he has for me, by his mere presence beside the President, unconscious that both were dogged by a midnight murderer, saved the life of General Garfield, on the night before the assassination was consummated. Mr. Secretary Blaine was with him at the time he was assassinated, and though he could not see the man behind, who dogged them both, took the chance involuntarily, and without a thought of personal danger to himself, of a ball missing, which might have then enter his back by pure mischance, instead of the back of President Garfield.

Again. At pages 1866–68, the responsibility was upon *President Garfield himself,* says the prisoner. He was the assassin.

If he had not, on the theory of the assassin, betrayed the men who elected him, counting Guiteau, who did not even vote for him, as one of them, he would not have died. The President, was responsible for his own death. "He betrayed the Republican party, and for this *he dies*."

We have the extraordinary statement, that Mrs. Garfield, the widow, whom so far as appears Mr. Reed never saw, has made him her private spokesman, to tell you that, while your deliberations are going on, she is absolutely kneeling in prayer, that you should find a verdict in favor of this poor, miserable, murdering lunatic. And he expects sworn jurors to accept his puerile and fanciful statement. There is a sense in which the prisoner makes *Mrs. Garfield* responsible for her husband's death. He swears, that when that honored lady, loved, as he impudently pretends, *by him*, leaned pale and feeble upon President Garfield's arm, for support, her presence did, for one day, nay more, for fourteen days, absolutely save his life. And, in that sense, she is responsible; for you will remember the significance of his answer, when I was cross-examining him and put this question : "If, on the second of July, while you held that bull-dog pistol in your hand, Mrs. Garfield had been by his side, would you have shot him?" "*I would not.*" This is the man who says he had *no choice*. This is the man who tells you that the power of the Deity was grinding, grinding, grinding with divine pressure, and that he would have committed this act of heartless and deliberate murder, though he had known that he would have been hanged by the mob for the crime, and would have perished the next minute. This lets you into the inside of the man. He would not in that case have killed him, *simply because he dared not*. And so Mrs. Garfield is made responsible for the death of her husband, by not being at his side on the second of July. Yet Mr. Reed would have you believe that the President's widow is praying for the man who shot him.

Gentlemen, they would have you also believe, that your moral nature should have been left outside when you came into the court room, and that you are bound to sit here as mere intellectual machines. Not so with the law. The judges are, really, in a certain sense to be intellectual machines. It is because they are so, at least in theory, that from a long time anterior to that *Magna Churta*, in which the learned gentleman supposes the trial by jury originated, from a time when our Anglo-Saxon ancestors sold their own white children as slaves, even from that time, *the jury of the vicinage* were always called in a case of murder, not only in England and its dependencies, but even in the forests of Germany and in the wilds of Scandanavia. The right of trial by jury existed, long before the charters granted by English kings. It originated when men felt, as you and I feel to-day, that a jury should be called, and a jury of the vicinage, and that they should bring with them their knowledge of men, and their abhorrence of crime, and that they should not leave their moral nature and their consciences outside when they enter the jury box.

You are asked to accept the statement of counsel, not attested, however, while he was on the witness stand, that Mrs. Garfield, while you are deliberating, is kneeling and praying that her husband's blood, which cries from the ground for justice, shall appeal to you in vain.

Gentlemen of the jury, what is the nature of the scenes which counsel has conjured up? I trust you appreciate the charity, which this praying Christian, through his counsel, now enjoins; the charity which would in other times have brought the victim's aged mother before you, and, in a room draped in black, as it would have been, if this cause had been tried, as it well might have been, in other times and other lands, the week following the murder; picture to yourselves that mother coming in this court room, according to the old custom of the English, to witness the trial in presence of the corpse, mutilated by the murderer, swathed in white linen, through which it was supposed of old, that the mere approach of the homicide would quicken the blood again to life, and mark him as the assassin; imagine General Garfield lying there—not merely one of the vertebræ of his backbone—but the whole man cold in death, and the death-sweat still lingering on his brow, with the expression of worn and weary agony which this prisoner had placed there, with the cowering actor in the drama shrinking from approach to the body—as in the old process of bier right—lest the blood in the winding sheet should indicate him as the assassin; and suppose that aged mother, who had looked to this son to close her eyes in death, bowed with grief at the coffin-head, with the widow, whose lips were the last that ever touched the cold lips of the dead President, sitting at his feet in dust and ashes. Suppose, in such a scene, the sympathetic counsel had stood up and announced to you, that the women who seemed to you kneeling only to God in sorrow, were really kneeling to Him to pray that the murderer might be delivered from justice!

Gentlemen, it is well for us all, that the law does not call on jurors to leave the only immortal part of their nature, their moral nature, at the court house door when they enter it to administer justice.

Well, Mrs. Garfield is responsible for this murder. But who else is responsible? As the prisoner would have you believe, *John H. Noyes.* He killed President Garfield. That John H. Noyes, from whom the prisoner stole the ideas put forth in his lectures on the second advent and the apostle Paul; and on that "hell," which was prominent in the first edition of his book, but which he changed to the milder form of "perdition" in the manuscript alterations—made as part of his preparations for the murder of the President.

Who else killed Garfield? *The prisoner's father*—that father whom he struck from behind, when he was eighteen years of age—that father whom he says he can never forgive—the father with whom he says, he was not on speaking terms for the last fifteen years of that honored life.

Who else is responsible? Who else killed Garfield? Why, *the mother* of the prisoner, whom he scarcely remembered, who was guilty of the

.nordinate atrocity of having a temporary attack of erysipelas, so severe that it required the cutting off of her hair, and who was in such infirm health, as to become the mother of three children in succession after him; but left to him an inheritance of "congenital monstrosity." She killed Garfield.

Who else? *Uncle Abraham*, the drunken and dissolute, but never insane, uncle. Though not insane himself, this uncle transmitted insanity to the prisoner. He was not his father nor his mother, nor his grandfather nor his grandmother; and though he did not become dissolute and drunken until after the prisoner was born, Uncle Abraham killed Garfield by making the prisoner insane.

Francis Guiteau, another uncle, being disappointed in love, fought a duel with his rival, in respect to which there are two versions by tradition, one that he killed the husband of the woman he loved, in vengeance for his own disappointment, and the other that he fought a sham duel, which exposed him to such ridicule and derision that it drove him long after into an insane asylum. He killed Garfield, by making this man the "congenital monstrosity," whom Dr. Spitka describes.

Then again. *Cousin Abby Maynard*, a bright, beautiful, brilliant girl, according to the account of all with whom she came in contact for years and years, but who unfortunately was taken possession of by one of the Guiteau order—a travelling mesmeriser—who by his experiments, robbed her of all that was attractive and engaging, and left her a wreck, so that afterwards a street boy, who is sought out somewhere, followed her and called her foolish Abby; but at last she was charitably taken by Mrs. Wilson to an asylum, where they receive those who are infirm of mind, as well as those who are insane. She, too, was responsible for the prisoner's becoming a "congenital monstrosity."

Who else committed this murder? Why, gentlemen, *the Chicago Convention*, by the nomination of President Garfield and Vice-President Arthur—they killed Garfield. They, too, were "inspired." His nomination was "an act of God." But if they had not selected him, the prisoner would not have killed him, and they are responsible.

Who else? *The electors of the United States*, Republican and Democratic—they killed Garfield. If they had not chosen him, the necessity would not have arisen. If they had not elected General Garfield, the idea is, that Guiteau would have got either the Austrian mission or the Paris consulship, and there would have been no occasion for the murder of President Garfield. He would not have been President. That too was "an act of God;" and inasmuch as God had, by two acts, made it necessary for him to kill General Garfield, he comes to the very natural conclusion, that when he determined to murder him, the Deity undertook to take the back track, and to correct his past errors, in inspiring the Chicago convention and the electors of the country into the nomination and election of

Garfield, and appointed HIM, HIM—HIM, with his swindling record; HIM, a broken-down lawyer; HIM, the man who fought his father, who lifted an axe at his sister, and struck his brother and benefactor; him, a sufferer by syphilis—HIM to correct the errors of Deity, by murdering the President, who had been elected by "an act of God!"

These are the sham defenses put forward by this praying prisoner and his counsel, in order to divert your attention from the fact that the man who killed President Garfield sits there—(pointing to the dock), and though Garfield is dead and mute, the prisoner speaks, and *has* spoken on the witness stand, those words which prove him to be a premeditated murderer —the deliberate, sane, and responsible assassin of the President.

But even these pretenses are not enough. *The press*—the press killed Garfield; and the press is summarily arraigned by the murderer and his counsel. It is indicted without the formality of a grand jury, accused by the oath of the homicide, and found guilty by the murderer. But unfortunately he no longer holds the bull-dog pistol in his hand, and the press can only be *convicted* of the murder of General Garfield by the blistered tongue of the false accuser. Is it really true, gentlemen, that we are not at liberty, through a free press, to declare our opinions as American freemen, on the policy of those who control the government? Is it true that when, in the heat of political controversy, we say hard things of each other—when in the earnestness and zeal of political contention, we array ourselves, one on one side and another on another, we are hoisting the black flag, and giving leave to murderers to kill those in whose policy we do not happen to concur? Is every member of a party or subdivision of a party, at liberty to advance its interests by shedding blood? That is, in this regard, the theory of the defense. Then comes, I am ashamed to say it, not from the prisoner, but from the senior counsel—his client having butchered Garfield as he would have slaughtered a calf that he desired to eat—a charge that three of our most eminent citizens are responsible for the act of this homicide. There are those, who are placed in too lofty a position, to be permitted to defend themselves against even the vipers that hiss at them. They would degrade their own dignity by noticing, or permitting any one else to notice, such a charge, with their concurrence. There is a distinguished American Senator, who would at this moment, were it not that he was already in too proud a position to justify his acceptance of the office, be sitting as Chief Justice of the United States—the son of a great and honored Federal jurist—a man, who though still young in years, has commanded more of the attention at home and abroad of the admirers of intellectual greatness, and of the highest order of eloquence and statesmanship, than almost any other man perhaps even of our time; an earnest, sincere and intense partisan; a man honest in all his utterances and all his acts. It has not been my fortune to have much intercourse with him in life; my time being engrossed in the duties of my profession, while he has been engaged in the more important and responsible duties of public life—a man faithful to his friends, and equally faithful to his convictions, even though fidelity involved sacrifice. He was capable of doing, what few men are, resigning the leadership in the Senate of the United States, second to no other parliamentary body in all Christendom, and to do it at the peril of his own political overthrow—a man not only of unstained integrity and honor, but of courage, fearlessness, and manliness, which made his withdrawal from the Senate a matter of regret even to his political adversaries—such a man is arraigned in his absence before an American jury, and arraigned not by the criminal, but by the criminal's defender, as responsible for the murder of President Garfield.

The Prisoner. Without my consent.

Mr. Porter. Again there is an honored "tanner," for so the counsel in his bitterness called him, a tanner of Galena, a tanner who is more honored to-day in the Confederate States than any American commander, save their own cherished leader, General Lee—a man more honored in the Northern States than any other citizen, who was nominated as a candidate for office from a feeling of earnest and sincere gratitude for services in war and afterwards in conciliation, a man whose life has been without dishonor or reproach, a man twice elevated by his countrymen to a most conspicuous position, as successor to the great office held by Washington and Jackson and Lincoln, and who, after he left that elevated position, was welcomed in every European and Oriental land, as second to none of the illustrious characters, whose names adorn the history of the nineteenth century. He is one of those arraigned by the lawyer of Guiteau——

The Prisoner. (Interjecting.) But not by Guiteau.

Mr. Porter. (Continuing)——as responsible for the murder of President Garfield. Nay, more than that; we have the present President of the United States——

The Prisoner. (Interjecting.) Made so by the inspiration of Guiteau.

Mr. Porter. (Continuing)——the successor of President Garfield, the successor of Lincoln, of Hayes, of Jackson, of Jefferson, of Adams, and Washington—elevated to that position, not by an assassin, but by the voice of his countrymen. Every vote in the United States which was cast for James A. Garfield was cast for Chester A. Arthur. It was cast with reference to the contingency of President Garfield's death. Every Democrat, and there were many thousands of them, or the ticket could not have been elected, every Republican, who voted for Garfield, voted also for the present honored President of the United States; and when this homicide says, "I made Arthur President," he forgets that General Arthur was made President by the voice of his countrymen; that he was made President by that very voice which made Garfield President, and in pursuance of the Constitution and the laws which provided for the contingency of death or disability, from whatever cause, of the nominee for the

Chief Magistracy. Millard Fillmore was just as truly elected by the people, as the President whom he succeeded.

The Constitution which was wiser, as has been said, than those who made it, foresaw the possibility of the death of the head of the nation and the disasters which might ensue, and provided for a simultaneous election of a successor in office.

The prisoner, in his speech, told you on Saturday, that the Constitution foresaw that Garfield might die any day, and from any cause, and that he might have slipped in treading upon an orange peel, and died of the resulting fall. So, too, he might have stepped upon a rattlesnake, and its fangs might have pierced his heel. Suppose either of these events had happened, would it be either the orange peel or the rattlesnake, that made General Arthur President?

The prisoner is shown by the evidence to have been all his life as slippery as the orange peel; all his life as venomous as the rattlesnake; but in one respect more dangerous, for Providence had provided in respect to that reptile, the earliest representative of the fiend, that he should give warning at one end, of the venom of death to be infused at the other. This was a rattlesnake without the rattle, but not without the fangs. The prisoner tells you that *he* made General Arthur President of the United States. He made him President, only in the same sense the snake would have done so, in the case supposed.

The counsel on the other side told you, in substance, that if you found a verdict, which should convict this man of murder it would be very horrible; *that General Garfield himself thought the man insane*, and would be shocked—this is the effect though not the language—at meeting him in that paradise, to which Guiteau's prayers and piety will undoubtedly conduct him, although he seems very averse to going there——

The PRISONER. (Interjecting.) That is a matter of opinion, sir.

Mr. PORTER. (Continuing.)——that when President Garfield meets him in that paradise, he is expected by counsel to express his astonishment, that a jury should have found guilty, that the Court should have sentenced, and that the law should have hung his murderer. Gentlemen, I adopt as a part of my argument, what you have all read, but which I wish to recall to your attention, because it is historical, to indicate how Mr. Reed misstates the views of the late President. He makes an assertion which undoubtedly he believes. He tells you, also, that he loved Garfield. I never heard of the love being mutual, nor of anything to produce a mutuality of love; but as counsel, he chooses to pose before you as the friend of Garfield. I take it for granted that he had read the little book, which lies on almost every book-stand of the country, containing memorable sayings of Garfield during his struggle between life and death, sayings simple as childhood, guileless, frank, sincere, yet significant utterances, between

Guiteau's bullet and his own death. In one of his waking hours on the 11th of July, the President asked Miss Susan A. Edson, where Guiteau was. You remember that this was when he expected to recover. He then remarked, people would doubtless come to him some day, with a petition for the pardon of that man, and he wondered what he should do in a personal matter like that. Miss Edson told him she should think he would do nothing at all. He certainly could not pardon such a man; and the President said, "*No, I do not suppose I could.*" Yet in his name, Mr. Reed, to whom the American bar is indebted for the introduction to its ranks of the prisoner, Guiteau, undertakes to say that the President regarded him as an irresponsible lunatic, and pictures his wife then, his widow now, as kneeling and praying, that when the jury come to pass upon the criminality of the murderer, they would act upon what? The example of the Saviour, who had the power, which you have not, of *forgiving crime*. It is astonishing what vital piety pervades and surrounds the dock. Mr. Reed, quietly assuming insanity, withdrawing from you the question whether this man was a lunatic, and deciding that for himself, gravely assures you, in substance and effect, that the Saviour of mankind was not in favor of hanging lunatics, and instead of that He cured them; that you, though mere mechanical machines, who have left your consciences and your moral nature outside the court-house, are to extend mercy to the homicide, on the theory that the Saviour would have done so. The passage which he cited—I remember its general tenor, although I do not recall the words—was inapt, by that singular fatality which has followed this man from the depot where he shed Garfield's blood, down to the dock where he stands to-day awaiting the verdict and sentence of the law. No one doubts the power of the Saviour of mankind to heal the sick, to forgive the sinner, to restore the lunatic, to purge and cleanse and purify the impure of heart. You are not gifted with that power of working miracles, but the Saviour, *in the very passage* from which counsel read, made the just distinction between the sick, the lunatic, and those possessed with devils. The claim in the present case is, that this man was so enormously wicked as to be, in the language of Dr. Spitzka, an absolute "moral monstrosity." He represents the distinctive class, of whom the Saviour spoke, *not as lunatics*, but as *possessed with devils*. But it is worth while to remember, what we are all familiar with, the mode in which He dealt, as we elsewhere learn, with those thus possessed. I do not at the moment recall the precise reference. It occurs in the record of the Evangelists; and I think the fullest version is in Mark. A man was brought to him, who was possessed with devils, and prayed to be delivered from them, a prayer which I am afraid has never arisen from the prisoner's dock, or from the prisoner before he entered it. The Saviour granted the prayer, and commanded the devil to announce his character. "My name is Legion, Legion." If you had the power of working a miracle, and could bring out the demoniac spirit which possesses this man, you would all be agreed that, upon the evidence, the *name* of the spirit was the same. The Saviour commanded—what you would command in vain—that the legion should come out of him. At His command they came out, and—for even devils go through the form of prayer—prayed to the Saviour that they might enter into a herd of swine ; and He suffered them. What became of the swine after the legion had entered them ? They rushed down into the sea. Whether the devil that possesses this man, is or is not to be choked by the mandate of the law, is for you in part to determine, but the ultimate destination of the swine, thus possessed, was to be choked in the waters of the sea. Gentlemen, I have said all that I deem necessary, on these side topics. We are here for the purpose of ascertaining whether *this man* is guilty, and these collateral issues as to the alleged guilt of others I shall not discuss, further than is needful incidentally, in the course of the general argument as to his personal criminality. It is, however, a mistake to suppose that you are—as in one of these *ad captandum* arguments you have been told, in the spirit of obsequious flattery--"twelve kings and emperors." Does such fulsome adulation commend itself to your sense of propriety ? Had it a motive ? What was it ? If I should use such language, I trust you would treat it with scorn. It is used, however, by the junior counsel of the prisoner, on whose certificate Guiteau was admitted to the bar, and who seems to have been the only man among our fifty millions, who could be induced to recommend him for office.

You are no more kings, gentlemen, than Messrs. Scoville and Reed are kings. There is an abstract sense, in which it is said, that as all sovereign power is wielded with us by the people, every American is a sovereign. But here, and for the purposes of this trial, you are told that each of you is not merely a sovereign but an emperor. There was a purpose in it. If it had come from Mr. Scoville, I might not have thought it an ingenuous purpose. As it comes from Mr. Reed, I can only think that they did not teach him his lesson well. Would he seriously lead you to suppose, that you can properly override the Judge and the law; that you are at liberty to disregard the instructions of the Court, and find your verdict, or refuse to find it, on the ground of speculative doubts, not warranted by the evidence, but based, as counsel suggests, *upon your own view of the prisoner*, or upon evidence which has not been submitted to you, but has been *excluded by the Court.*

At this point, 12 o'clock m., the Court took a recess until half past 12.

AFTER RECESS.

Mr. PORTER. At the recess I was calling your attention to the fact, that Mr. Reed in the opening argument exalted you into "kings and emperors," seemingly in the hope of thus inveigling you into overlooking your oaths and in disregard of the evidence given, acting upon speculation founded on your own view, and on evidence not given by either side. It seemed to me that while this was a fulsome and inappropriate suggestion to be made to a jury, it was one which should call your attention to the differing responsibility of sworn jurors and unsworn counsel. As I said before recess, either of you is a king, only in the same sense in which the prisoner is a king, as he sits in his box uncrowned, except in his own conceit. He evidently supposes, that when he has qualified himself to lift hands stained with illustrious blood, he has made himself illustrious; that it is for him to award immortality to you, to his counsel, and the Judge. Indeed, he frankly intimates, that your names will be dishonored if you respect your oaths, and that the honored name of the Judge will be blasted, unless he comes to the rescue of the homicide, notwithstanding the sworn evidences of his guilt.

He cautiously warns the President, and other distinguished men of the republic, and even the Deity, that they must take heed how they deal with him. He condescends, however, to assure you that he is satisfied, *so far*, with what the Almighty has done, but intimates his modest expectation that before this trial is through, if it is necessary to shield him, this prayer-making innocent, you or I or the Judge will be struck down by direct interposition from above. All this is well played. He is not only a mimic, but an actor, and has shown it repeatedly through the progress of the trial. While in jail he has appeared in his real part. Here he has been constantly posing on the stage for your benefit, possibly in accordance with the suggestions of his counsel; and, by way of variety, he has occasionally indulged you with abuse of his senior counsel, which promoted the purpose of that counsel, and was not improbably a part of the programme. Gentlemen, he is neither a crowned nor an uncrowned king, notwithstanding his pretense of divine inspiration. He knows it; and though there are many here, men, women, and children of all races and nations, I venture to say, that though the prisoner claims to have been a divine agent in removing the President to paradise, and though he has repeatedly assured you that he was prepared to meet his God, there is probably not one soul in this assembly that shrinks with such abject cowardice from confronting the Deity to whom he appeals.

Gentlemen, Mr. Reed is mistaken. It would be no credit to you to be kings and emperors. If you had been, your will would have been your law; and that was the moral of Mr. Reed's argument—that, for this purpose, you were clothed with *imperial irresponsibility*, and could determine, without regard to the evidence or the law, upon your own view, whether this man was or was not an insane homicide. Kings and emperors are, to some extent, a law unto themselves. It is the boast of every American citizen, that he recognizes a governmental authority above his own, and bows, as a juror, to the law as declared by the Courts.

His honor is, here, the official exponent of the law, and for the purposes of the present trial, his ruling is binding and controlling. Kings, as we think, *are made by men*. Jurors, according to our theory of the law, are *made by God*, and it is in His image that they act and speak. They have, and should have, human sympathies. They have the sense of conscience, of duty, and of just indignation at wrong. They have, and should have, the intelligence to see the right, and the integrity to uphold and enforce it. Believing, as I do, from the close observation of each man of your number, one by one, through these weary eleven weeks—forming the best judgment I could of your characters—I venture to affirm that the prisoner is mistaken, and that there is not an unworthy juror in that box, that there is no man-made king, no man-made emperor; that you are God-made men. The result will show whether this judgment is right.

Gentlemen, after having disposed of those outlying and incidental portions of the argument of the three gentlemen, which seem to me to call for particular observation, I come to the real issue, which is not one of general inquisition, but of direct and personal accusation. Did *this man* murder General Garfield, and did he know what he was doing, and that in so doing he was violating divine and human law? If he did, then, as I understand the law, as adjudged by this Court, he is responsible. I have abstracted from the original rulings, what I think a full and fair epitome of the views, of his honor. If I have failed to do so, the Court will correct me. Legal forms, gentlemen, are often entangling and confusing. Laymen, who are necessarily unfamiliar with them, may often be misled by technical phraseology, without the explanations given in the final charge to the jury. His honor's rulings cover many pages of this record. You are to accept them. The *prisoner* has a right of appeal from them, but *you have none*. The oath you have taken, binds you just as much to receive the instructions of his honor, on questions of law, as if there were not another Judge on the face of the earth, and to pass on these issues as he shall submit them to you, in accordance with the legal rules of evidence. The first of those issues is:

Was Charles J. Guiteau *insane* on the 2d of July, 1881? If he was not, the case is at an end; and the deliberate homicide being undisputed, your sworn duty is to convict him.

Second. If he was *not* sane on that day, was he insane *to such a degree* that he did not know that the homicide was morally and legally wrong? If he was not insane *to that degree*, you are bound by your oaths under the law, to find him guilty.

Third. If, in disregard of his confessions, and the other evidence, you should find, that he actually and honestly *believed* that God had commanded him to assassinate the President, and was thus under a delusion, unless you find the further fact that such delusion existed *to such an extent* as to disable him from knowing that the act was morally and legally wrong, you are bound, by your oaths, to convict him.

Fourth. If you find that such delusion did exist, that God *had* so commanded him, and that delusion was one resulting from *actual insanity*, then you are at liberty to acquit him, if you find that such insane delusion existed to such a degree that he was *unable to control his own will*. In that connection, bear in mind that he has sworn to the fact, that he was able to control his own will, and that if *Mrs. Garfield* had been at the side of the President he would have controlled it, and the President would have lived to see the sun set on the 2d of July, untouched by the mortal wound.

Fifth. If you find that, even though he was partially insane, the delusion was one *resulting from his own conception in the beginning*, his own subsequent reasoning, his own contrivance and craft, and his own malignity and depravity, notwithstanding he thus came really to entertain such insane delusion *as a result of his criminal and wicked purpose*, still you are bound, under the instructions of the Court, to hold him criminally responsible.

Sixth. If upon the whole case you have no reasonable doubt, that whether he was partially insane or wholly sane, *he knew* that the killing of the President was legally and morally wrong, you are bound by your oaths, and under the instructions of the Court, as to the law, to hold him responsible for his act.

(To the Court.) May I pass this memorandum up to your honor? (Handing same to Court.) Because I desire you to see——

MR. REED. (Interposing.) That is what you propose to ask the Court to instruct the jury.

THE COURT. That is his construction upon what the Court has already said.

MR. REED. Very well.

MR. PORTER. His honor will charge you at the close of the argument upon all the questions involved. I have endeavored to present fully and fairly the instructions of the Court as I understand them. They are not in the precise form in which Mr. Davidge submitted them, but they are, in the main, in substantial accordance with most of those which he submitted, and I have endeavored, perhaps imperfectly, to express every qualification that the Judge felt it important and proper to make, in order to prevent unjust inferences from his charge in this or in future cases. These are the prominent issues. I begin with the first of them. If I have made them intelligible, you will see that they are so intermingled in the evidence, that I can not undertake to separate it with reference to each. If, however, you follow my argument, you will see that on each of these propositions we are furnished with evidence, from the effect of which there is no escape.

It is no abstract question—*who* killed President Garfield? It is the direct question whether *this man* killed him; whether, if he did, he was sane or insane; whether, if insane, he was so to such a degree that he did not know legal and moral right from wrong in respect of this act; and if he did, whether he was disabled by insane delusion which mastered his self-control, so that when he put his finger to that trigger, he could not have controlled it, even if Garfield's wife had hung on his arm, and his children had been clinging to his skirts. The issue is of momentous importance and gravity. You will see why it must be so. If men like the prisoner were irresponsible, who would be safe? What household would be secure? What church would protect its worshipers, even with the aid of the law? Is it true, that every man who has unfortunately had an insane cousin, an insane aunt, or some insane ancestor, though sane himself to the extent of knowing perfectly, that murder is legally and morally wrong, holds your life and mine, and those of our sons and daughters, and our wives, in the hollow of his right hand? If such a man may stab, shoot, waylay and murder you, in any form, by day or by night, and his sufficient vindication shall be, not that he is insane, but that *somebody else was*, what is the security of human life? Nay more, if it were true that every insane man—for that is the doctrine of the counsel on the other side—no matter in what degree; no matter whether from temporary melancholia, or any of those casual and occasional aberrations of mind to which all are subject, and which, as one of Guiteau's witnesses would have you believe, embraces ten millions of people in the United States, one-fifth of the entire population—exceeding that of any two States in the Union—if it be true, that all these men are licensed to murder you and yours, they are equally licensed to forge your name, to enter your house by midnight burglary, to stab your wife as she sleeps by your side, to force your strong box and seize your money and your bonds, to fire your dwelling, to set Washington City in flames, to poison your wells, to ravish your daughters. This is the nature of the license, for which the counsel for the prisoner contends. The law is obligatory, on this theory, only on those who are *perfectly* rational. True, no such license is given by the law, but it is to be established by "a jury of twelve emperors" in defiance of the law, and of the courts who declare it. Nay, more; the insane of this country are to learn from the verdict asked from this jury—I mean the actual and undoubted insane—the inmates of lunatic asylums, consigned to seclusion by operation of law—that each one of them is at liberty to kill the keepers who restrain his liberty; every one of them may unite with a sufficient number of others, to open the gates of each asylum, and go out, knife and torch in hand, to spread ruin and conflagration. The law forbids such acts, and no American jury can be found to sanction them. More than this; on this new-fangled theory, every man who is insane, in any degree, is at liberty to slaughter *any other insane man*. In the mercy of a good Providence, we have not as yet been inmates of a lunatic asylum, but there is no one in this great audience, who is not exposed to such a calamity. The case may occur, in which our friends, our own families, may lawfully consign either of us to a lunatic asylum. Brought by misfortune, by no fault of ours, into association with a hundred or a thousand lunatics, every one of them is at liberty, on this new theory, to take our lives. If such were the law, gentlemen, these benign institutions—asylums for the insane—must be practically abandoned. Let insane men as a class, understand that the law has no hold upon them, and that they can commit with impunity all acts prohibited as crimes—and no troops in the command of General Sherman could so guard our asylums, as to protect the lives of the inmates from each other, or of the keepers from the inmates. Probably nowhere did this man's crime produce more horror than in these asylums. Assassination can look for no favor there. I do not doubt that if a jury could be impaneled in any insane asylum in this country, they would regard this man, not only as one whose presence would endanger them, but as one who had proved himself unfit to live.

The law, gentlemen, is founded upon reason. I ought not to be called upon to commend it to your deference and respect, for it is enough that it is announced as your controlling rule of action in the present case by the eminent jurist who presides in this tribunal.

If this were a civil case, I should discuss no question beyond the single one of the entire sanity of the prisoner. It seems to me to be established beyond all controversy. But as a capital crime is charged, I must go further; for, whatever may be my views, some juror may entertain doubt. It will be necessary, therefore, to consider somewhat fully the general evidence in the cause. But, first, was he insane on the 2d of July? If he was not, you have but one duty, and that is, to convict him. We claim that he was not insane. Grant, for the purpose of the argument, what I am confident not one soul of you believes, that his father was insane. His father did not assassinate President Garfield. Grant, if you please, what no one believes, that his uncle Abram was insane. His uncle Abram is not on trial, and did not murder the President. Grant the same of each and all his collateral relatives. None of them shot General Garfield. The prisoner did. Was *he* insane on that day? We aver that he never was insane, and certainly not on the 2d of July. The principal basis of the contrary claim is the atrocity, and the foolhardiness of this particular act. This is persistently urged by the prisoner from the dock. I do not deny his title, to be regarded as the most cold-blooded and selfish murderer of the last sixty centuries. Certainly there was atrocity enough. But he is not alone in this, as he may find, if he ever reaches the supposed realm where murderers are said to "herd together." *The first-born of the human race murdered the second-born;* and though the corpse was mute, the blood appealed from the ground to that God, who set upon the brow of the homicide the mark which doomed him to live thus branded—a punishment then more terrible than death.

Murder is a crime which has existed in all ages. We speak of one *man*, as knowing more than another, of human nature. There is one who knows *more of it than all of* us, and speaking four thousand years ago to the whole human race, then living and thereafter born, and knowing that from cupidity, from passion, from diabolic hate, from the thousand causes within his prevision, man would be tempted to shed the blood of his brother man, He inscribed on tables of stone, committed to the keeping of a chosen and ancient people, the commandment :

Thou shalt not kill.

Human life is differently estimated by Guiteau. "Life," says he, in his letter of consolation to the widow, "is a fleeting dream, and it matters little when one goes. A human life is of small value." *That is all Cain took.* As he told you the other day, Garfield might have slipped upon an orange peel. He who moulded each of us in his image, entertained different views of the value of his own handiwork :

Whoso sheddeth man's blood, by man shall his blood be shed.

The PRISONER. That was said three or four thousand years ago. *That is old.*

Mr. PORTER. (Continuing.) And the prisoner in the dock tells you he believes that the God, *who never grows old*, and who placed that value on human life, placed none on the life of James A. Garfield, and as to that handed it over to this swindling lawyer to be dealt with as a fleeting dream. We have had the gospel of Guiteau, and he thinks you will indorse it. You see what is the Gospel of Him who created us all, and before whom each of us is to stand in judgment *severally*, and answer for the observance or the defiance of His supreme law.

It is said this man is *insane by inheritance.* From whom did he inherit it ? From a homicide ? *From a murderer ?* No. He inherited it, as he claims, from *the father*, who reverently worshipped God down to the day of his death ; from the father who, through all his honored life, was recognized by the community in which he lived as a pure, upright, conscientious and truthful man. He inherited it from the father, at whose bedside his own witness, Dr. Rice, stood in the last hours of his life. He had been his attending physician ; he knew him well and intimately, and he testifies that *he had never been insane ; never, never.* You have the oath of the prisoner's brother, who slept in the same womb from which he came, until that sleep was awakened into life. This brother swears that their father never was insane. You have the evidence of the sister, who came from the same womb, and Mr. Scoville did not venture to put to his own wife the question, whether Luther W. Guiteau was insane. If he was insane, his family physician knew it ; his oldest son knew it ; his daughter knew it ; her husband, Mr. Scoville knew it. None of them has testified that they, or either of them, believed Luther W. Guiteau to be insane.

Was *the prisoner's mother* insane? Not one human being affirms it; not even the assassin. Going back to the *grandparents, and their grandparents*, there is not even a family tradition, that any of those whose blood mingled in his veins was ever a lunatic. More than that, you have clear and conclusive evidence, that if Luther W. Guiteau had murdered the President of that day, had waylaid him, had planned six weeks the means of safely killing him; had been, like this man, a baffled and disappointed office-seeker, he could not have interposed the pretense of insanity. The defense is a falsehood and a fabrication. It is a sham and an imposture. But gentlemen, I do not deny, that there is another species of *hereditary* tendency to insanity, which the prisoner calls *Abrahamic insanity*.

The Prisoner (Interjecting.) I am glad to hear you say it, Mr. Porter.

Mr. PORTER. (Continuing.) It is described by him at other times as temporary mania, by Dr. Spitzka as moral insanity or congenital monstrosity; but better by that most eminent scientist, Dr. Barker, as simple wickedness. It is *inherited*, not from the *natural parent*, but from another source. I reminded you yesterday, of the rebuke of the Saviour to the scribes and Pharisees:

Those who are of the seed of Abraham prove it by doing the works of Abraham; but ye are *the children of your father the devil*, who was a murderer from the beginning.

That is the order of *hereditary* insanity, which he has derived from the source, laid bare by the Saviour of mankind, and of which you see so striking an illustration in the prisoner's dock. What is insanity? You have heard the evidence, and you have heard the authorities. Insanity is a *disease of the brain*. On that all substantially agree. Even Dr. Spitzka concurs in this. As I understand him, it is a product of disease of the brain. The first question, then, is, was the man's brain diseased on the 2d of July? We are relieved from any very extended discussion upon that point. If his brain was diseased, it was a singularly curable and evanescent disease. It *left him in the same hour in which he assassinated the President*. At one time in his examination, it is true, he claimed that he was legally insane from the first day of June. His brain became diseased on that day, and it was cured on the second of July, when he had lodged that bullet in the vitals of the President. That is the species of disease of the brain this man had. He leaves you to infer, that if on the 16th of June, when he first wrote "I have shot the President," it has been true, and time and tide had favored him, this disease of the brain would have been cured on that day. If it had happened that Mrs. Garfield had not been leaning on the President's arm on the 18th of June, his curiously accommodating disease of the brain would have been cured at that date. If, on the subsequent day, when he saw the President leave the White House for a ride to the Soldier's Home, in company with some friends, he had happened to be sitting in the carriage *alone*, his disease of the brain would have evaporated into thin air on that day. If on the subsequent occasion, when he went, prayerfully prowling about that inconspicuous place of worship, in order to remove the President gently with his bull-dog bullet to paradise, there had not been *so many Christians present*, and no hackman ready at the door to hurry him to the jail for protection, his disease of the brain would have disappeared on that Sabbath day. If on the night of the 1st of July, President Garfield had chanced to come out *alone* from Secretary Blaine's house, his disease of the brain would have been spontaneously cured that night. As it was, it lasted until the 2d of July, when he planted that bull-dog bullet in the backbone of the President. Then, according to his account, *it left him*. This is the issue, which he thinks he can safely submit to you. For this purpose I lay out of view all evidence except his own. He has made it evident that he is a liar, as well as an assassin, and that he was instigated to this foul act, not by the Almighty, but by the father of liars.

But let us go further, gentlemen. Is it not a little extraordinary, that a man who has a disease of the brain, is one who, according to his own policy of life insurance, as well as his own evidence, and his statements to the physicians, never had a serious illness of any sort in his life, never had a physician, and never suffered from sickness except in jail, and that merely by malaria and indigestion, produced by overfeasting at one of his thanksgiving levees? We find a man in perfect health now, as every physician who has examined him testifies, who has suffered in the past no ailment, except one, originating in his blasphemous rendering of the commandment, "Thou shalt not commit adultery,"—from which he seems to have recovered without the aid of a physician—who claims to have been suddenly overtaken on the 1st of June with a disease of the brain, yet continued to live at a "high-toned boarding house" at the expense of the proprietress; did not pay a dollar for his board; was punctual in taking his baths; punctual at breakfast, at dinner, at tea; punctual at night: slept well, ate heartily, rose early, and spent the day at Lafayette square, or in making preparations elsewhere to murder the President, when he found a favorable opportunity to butcher him *alone*. This he calls *temporary mania; Abrahamic mania*. This is the peculiar disease of the brain, which resulted in a political murder, for the ostensible benefit of the stalwarts of the Republican party.

The PRISONER. For the benefit of the American people, sir. A *removal* and not a murder. They are well satisfied with it, too.

Mr. PORTER. Gentlemen, if I went no further, do you believe that this man's brain was diseased on the 2d of July? I deal with nothing else now. Was his brain diseased, and did the disease come and go, just as it happened that President Garfield went out alone, or with his wife, or with his children, or drove to the Soldiers' Home, or rode to the railway depot? Do you believe that the right remedy for a disease of the brain is, to make six weeks' preparation for shooting another man through the spine? Yet with him, it proved a perfect and effectual cure. That is the case as he presents it. But, gentlemen, in what other aspects is this matter presented for your consideration? I should remind you, because it is worthy of note, that this pretense of insanity did not originate with Mr. Scoville, but with the prisoner, who now more than half disclaims it. He was engaged for six weeks in making preparation for the murder of Garfield, and *for his own safety* against the natural consequences of the act. He did not wish to be removed to paradise with President Garfield. He was a Christian man, a theologian, a praying man, and while he prayed that Garfield might be removed, he prayed with still more earnest fervor that he might be preserved from sharing his fate. He provided, first, for a hackman, to save him from the indignation of the community, for an act of atrocious legal and moral wrong, which he knew would subject him to the peril of instant death. He was a lawyer, and he had carefully prepared his defense. What was that defense, as first proposed? That his killing was no murder, for he had no *malice*. In the very hour of the murder, that mock defense was to be on its way over the telegraph wires, not only in this country, but also beneath the ocean and to other lands. In effect it was this:

I had no malice. This is not an act of murder, but of patriotic devotion.

He had, however, gone farther in his preparations than that. He did not publish his further devices in his papers then, but *he had pre-arranged another alternative defense*. It was in substance this:

I thought I was *legally* insane, but not in fact insane. That was my opinion during this period of preparation. I knew that many men had called me a crank; and a crank is one who is very insane. I knew that I could prove it by fifty physicians, if I had money enough to get them; *for physicians can easily be bought*. I shall have money enough for that purpose, but I shall be conferring a benefit upon the Stalwart party, which will promptly and gladly respond to the first ring of my bell, and when I call upon the beneficiaries to contribute, the checks will roll in upon me for hundreds and thousands.

This was plainly his pre-arranged alternative.

He neglected *no other* precaution for his own safety, and if he overlooked *this, it was evidently the only precaution he neglected*. But he did not overlook it, and he admits it. Legal insanity! murder without malice! patriotic murder! Gentlemen, you see that from the beginning, he was apprehensive that he might be driven to this defense, and he provided for it. How it happened, that so soon after the murder, and within 48 hours, he was in consultation with his leading counsel, we do not know.

We do know, that from the Sunday or Monday, I do not remember which, when Mr. Scoville arrived, the press of the country has been burdened with allegations of the prisoner's insanity.

The PRISONER. Mr. Scoville called as a friend, and not as counsel.

Mr. PORTER. Undoubtedly; but it was an opportune call, when the prisoner needed it.

The PRISONER. Nothing was said about my defense, until after I was indicted.

Mr. PORTER. I thought Mr. Scoville intimated that there was something said about his defense, and that the claim of inspiration was made in his presence; and I have waited to see him come forward and swear to it, but have waited in vain.

The PRISONER. Because he is my counsel. Mr. Brooks swore to it, sir. Corkhill and Bailey got the information in the note-book on the 2d or 3d of July, and it was suppressed.

Mr. PORTER. I shall, in due time, come to Mr. Brooks. Again, on this question of insanity, there is a most excellent test. If he was ever insane, there was a time when he became so. This man had led a vagrant and an idle life. If he was insane somebody knew it. All his life he had been among other men, and he knew who they were. Certainly he has a more remarkable memory than any other man I ever saw, either in or out of court. He knew who they were, and he has had the benefit of process to subpœna anybody and everybody, by the authority of the government and at its expense, a thing which, though authorized here by local law, was never before done in any country in the world, so far as I have heard.

The PRISONER. I have had about one-third as many witnesses as the prosecution has, sir.

Mr. PORTER. He has produced all he could find. Now, who are those who would be likely to know, and to know best? One was the father who begot him. He is dead, and in a spirit of fairness to the prisoner, we permitted the production in evidence of a letter of the dead father, not otherwise admissible. I shall recur to this letter again. Another witness was his living sister. She has been sworn. I shall have occasion to refer to her testimony. Another was his brother-in-law, George W. Scoville. I am sorry to say that I shall *not* be able to refer to his testimony. For some reason it has not been given. The man most competent to speak chooses to do so without the rigid restraint of an oath.

The PRISONER. He is my counsel, sir, and it would not be proper for him to be a witness.

Mr. PORTER. Another, John W. Guiteau, his brother, has spoken, and has told you that, knowing him from the time he came from his mother's womb, down to a period after the President's death, his conviction *then was* that he was perfectly sane, but that he was instigated by the devil.

The PRISONER. He is not my reference, and has not known anything about me for twenty years. That is the kind of a brother he has been to me. I have got first-class men as references.

Mr. PORTER. There is one other witness, who better than all else ought to know whether he was sane or insane. That is the woman who loved him.

The PRISONER. (Interjecting.) I did not love her.

Mr. PORTER. (Continuing.) Few have loved him.

The PRISONER. (Interjecting.) It was a one-sided affair.

Mr. PORTER. (Continuing.) The woman who married him.

The PRISONER. (Interjecting.) That was a swindle.

Mr. PORTER. (Continuing.) The woman who slept with him.

The PRISONER. (Interjecting.) Sometimes she did and sometimes she didn't.

Mr. PORTER. (Continuing.) The woman who borrowed for him; the woman who gave the earnings of her industry to furnish him with money, which he expended on street prostitutes, the woman whose divorce was obtained by his procurement——

The PRISONER. (Interjecting.) I did not love her, and I have no business to have married her.

Mr. PORTER. (Continuing)——and by such dastardly meanness and ignominy that it horrifies one even to name it, in connection with the fact that he and the adulteress were witnesses in the proceeding for "removing" his wife.

The PRISONER. That happened about ten years ago, and has nothing to do with this case one way or the other.

Mr. PORTER. (Continuing.) Gentlemen, these are the men and women *who ought to know* whether he was sane or insane, and when he became so. Let us see whom he has called. The men whom he cheated and swindled, those whom he defrauded into furnishing him with lecture rooms and procuring advertisements for him, those who were disgusted with his blasphemies and his egotism, when he delivered the stolen lectures, which he claimed were the work of inspiration. Such witnesses he called. He also called a Dr. Rice, who has been the physician of his father.

The PRISONER. (Interjecting.) I never saw Rice but two or three times in my life; know nothing about him; and care nothing about him.

Mr. PORTER. (Continuing.) He never saw him but two or three times in his life. He says so, and it is probably true. It is confirmed by what Dr. Rice says, of what occurred on those two or three occasions when he casually saw him. This gentleman is brought here to prove, that the prisoner was insane on the 2d of July, 1881, *five years after they met and parted.* Of his sanity on the 2d of July, Dr. Rice knew no more than you or I did; but it did appear from his testimony, that an incident occurred in the year 1876, of which the doctor was *not a witness*, but which was reported to him by his sister, in connection with the lifting of that ax against her life.

The PRISONER. *That never took place.*

Mr. PORTER. He also testifies to an incident, not improbable, in connection with his accustomed outbreaks after the manner of the Oneida Community, which occurred in a private house where he casually met him, and led him to suspect his insanity.

The PRISONER. (Interjecting.) The kind that Dr. Barker talked about— *transitory mania ; that is all I claim.*

Mr. PORTER. (Continuing.) Dr. Rice describes it as insanity *without delusion, without hallucination and without illusion*, in other words, *without disease of the brain.* It was a curious order of insanity which did not lead the doctor even to sign a certificate, *as he was asked to do.* It was insanity of a kind which did not lead the doctor to confer with another physician as required by law, and in respect of which Mrs. Scoville frankly says in her testimony that if the doctor did tell her the things he swears to now, *she did not so understand it.* Dr. Rice's testimony has been commented upon so much that I need not read it in full, but the fact that he swore that Luther W. Guiteau was *not insane* may not now be fresh in your recollection. Perhaps I had better read a little of the context, as the prisoner says the doctor never saw him but twice or three times. It was in June or July, 1876. Mrs. Scoville at first got the date wrong, but it was afterwards corrected, and this was undoubtedly due to her defect of memory. She had not the dates fresh in mind. The only fact beyond what Mrs. Scoville stated—and of that I shall speak presently—with regard to his insanity, was this :

I saw him during an ordinary evening conversation suddenly arise and appeal to those who were near him to come to the Lord.

Mr. SCOVILLE. From what page do you read?

Mr. PORTER. I was reading from page 353, at that time. I read further now in relation to the prisoner's father :

Q. Was Luther W. Guiteau, during the time that you attended him, deranged ?
The WITNESS. Insane ?
Mr. SCOVILLE. Yes ; out of his mind or whatever you call it.
A. *I do not think he was.*

That was true, even of the last days of his life, though the prisoner has alleged that his father was deranged for some considerable period before his death. I think he mentioned it as *six weeks.* At the bottom of page 355 Dr. Rice is asked :

Did you ever meet him (the prisoner) afterwards?—A. No, sir; I never met him since.
* * * * * * *

Q. State to the jury, if you know, about his leaving Colonel Shears—

That was where this extraordinary circumstance occurred, of his appeal to the bystanders, *in the Oneida Community fashion,* to come to the Lord. —or anything further connected with his conduct there?—A. I was informed that he borrowed *some clothing and disappeared all at once without paying for his board.*

That is the testimony set up as a defense for the murder of Garfield, *five years afterwards,* and this is the witness the prisoner and his brother-in-law, thought would be more useful to him than his sister Flora, than the other inmates of the house, than his step-mother, than all those who lived with him, than all those who knew him in his household relations. Then we have the ex-Unitarian minister who had retired, *perhaps for conscience sake,* into a gathering of those who, like Dr. Spitzka, did not care to acknowledge the Creator, that made them; or who, like Dr. Kiernan, did not believe in a future state of existence. I pass him, and others like him, because, of course, they did not in any just sense *know him,* and had no means of forming an intelligent opinion, either by personal acquaintance or otherwise. I come now to Mrs. Scoville, pausing for a moment to refer to the record.

The PRISONER. That gives me time to say that I am in receipt of a letter from a New York gentleman, who says he has conversed with two hundred and fifty intelligent people, and *that they are all of the opinion that the Almighty inspired my act.* I have a letter from a prominent gentleman in Maryland, a first-class lawyer, who says that I will go into history, by the side of Grant and Washington. That is their opinion of this matter.

Mr. PORTER. That is very good acting, gentlemen of the jury. I shall have to ask you to indulge me in reading some passages from Mrs. Scoville's evidence, because I believe her to be a sincere woman, and while I am not willing to adopt all her opinions, and I think you would not, yet the facts she states are well worth knowing, and considering. Her *opinions* are naturally biased, as I hope your sisters' or mine would be, if we were in peril of approaching death, and especially an ignominious death. In respect of her mother, she speaks of her principal difficulty as *neuralgia.* I hope none of you are so unfortunate as some of us are, as to be occasional sufferers from this complaint, but I am very sure that none of you will think it is a very marked indication of insanity. The mother was seriously ill at one time, and her hair was cut off, as one among other remedial agencies often resorted to in ordinary fevers, and in other inflammatory diseases. It is one of the known and approved methods of cooling the head when it is heated by the delirium of fever or by other temporary causes, and it often gives relief to the patient. It is not regarded as an evidence of, or a remedy for, insanity. The length of the hair is not supposed to indicate, or to affect very materially the condition of the brain in respect of sanity. Mr. Reed has given you to understand that the prisoner, down to the time he entered the Oneida Community, was a perfectly moral, pure, gentle, kindly, and dutiful boy. *Is this true?* What becomes of that bold and reckless allegation, which rests upon his own statement, and Mr. Scoville's unsworn indorsement, that when he was a boy he was struck in a school-boy encounter with a stone, which penetrated so deeply into the skull that you could introduce your finger now, half an inch into the hole.

The PRISONER. *That did not happen to take place, sir.*

Mr. PORTER. I know it did not, and I was sure it was a fiction when the plaster cast was produced——

The PRISONER. (Interjecting.) I never said anything about it, sir.

Mr. PORTER. (Continuing)——and when the doctor swore that there was not only *no cavity* on that side of his head into which you could introduce your finger half an inch, but none into which you could introduce your finger *at all*——

The PRISONER. (Interjecting.) Yes there is.

Mr. PORTER. (Continuing)——and that the scar to which he refers is one of *a scalp wound simply.*

The PRISONER. It is about a sixteenth of an inch, and you can see it.

Mr. PORTER. The doctor and the prisoner, as usual, disagree. It was paraded before you in the opening that he was a good, moral, sane, intelligent, and bright boy until he came to be 19 years of age. Of course, in quoting the language of counsel, I do so only, according to the effect and import of his statement. I do not profess to give his precise words, for it would take me too long to turn to the particular passages. You know the impression the argument was intended to convey to you.

We come to another extraordinary statement of Mr. Reed, by way of accounting for his alleged insanity. This boy lived, as counsel tells you, six years, and was still unable to talk. Again and again in his argument he repeated this, as a strong circumstance tending to show that there was some deficiency in the boy, and some predisposition to insanity. *He could not talk!* He was sent to school to learn *to talk.* He had lived six years without being able to speak the name of his father or his mother, or to express his ordinary wants! The amiability, the morality, the excellence of this boy, and *his inability to talk* are based on page 463 of Mrs. Scoville's evidence. What she says is :

I remember that he was very active, and what you would call a troublesome child, because he was so very active.

He has kept up that character ever since, as President Garfield learned to his cost.

That is the main thing I can remember about his babyhood. *He was very precocious; very smart.*

How did she find that out, from a boy *that couldn't talk?*

He seemed to be able to make enough noise in every other way, but he could not talk *plain* so that anybody could understand him.

Q. State to the jury *any instances* that you remember of his failure to talk.

Then she goes on to say, he had the fever and ague, and during that time he used to lie down on the floor behind the stove. Of course, you know that children with fever and ague ought hardly to be called insane, because they put themselves, when cold, in a position where they can get warmth. I do not think that is a very controlling evidence of insanity.

At these times—

And you will remember, this was when he was but five years old—

he would invariably lie down behind the stove and *would sing his little song,* " *Ped along, Old Dan Tucker*"—

A boy who *couldn't talk*, but *could sing* his habitual song!—

whenever he had these chills. I remember that my father got provoked because he would not speak *plain.*

Was a father ever provoked with his child because he could not talk? Oh, no; but in this instance it was because he *would* not speak *plain.*

He would say "Ped along," and would not say anything else. He could not say any of it plain, but that word in particular was very peculiar.

He would say "ped" for "come." Well, it was a song, which he had learned while he was younger, and having that lisp in the tongue which is so common with children, and being unable to pronounce c or q at the period when he learned the song, he, *as a lisping boy,* substituted "ped along" to avoid a difficulty of articulation, which made him, when he spoke of quail, that abounded around his father's house, call them "pail;" and *this childish and lisping utterance* is gravely put forward as evidence that on the 2d of July 1881, when he, being forty years of age, murdered the President, he must have been insane, because thirty-five years before, when he was a boy, chilled by fever and ague, he crept behind the stove in the rigor of his chills, and sung his little song, substituting "ped along" for "come along," and this is seriously urged to you, in order that you may not recognize *the color of the bloody hands* he now holds up to you.

At all events, *his father ought to know* something of this unexampled proof of insanity. It is true that his father when the boy persisted in saying "pail" for "quail," immediately punished him. He became provoked one day, and said he knew the boy *could talk plain, if he chose to make the effort*, and the father chastised him; whereat Mrs. Scoville, then a little girl, was greatly shocked. The father, more competent than her to judge, thought it was *from perverseness in the child*. He thought there was no actual impediment of speech, but the boy would not, or did not correct the habit, and in the end he was kindly sent to school where he at once got over it. I never heard before of a boy being sent to school to learn to *talk*, and I do not think you ever heard such a trivial and childish incident magnified into a theme of forensic eloquence, as being clear and cogent evidence that a lisping boy was born utterly irresponsible and with a general and plenary *license to murder*, derived from defect of perfect utterance when he was a mere child. In regard to dates, Mrs. Scoville states that she was married the 1st of January, 1852 or 1853, she did not remember which. There are few ladies who forget the day they were married, but you perceive that in respect to dates, her memory is by no means clear. It sometimes happens with people of the highest intelligence and integrity, that they are unable to recall dates with accuracy and precision. She makes one or two unimportant mistakes, which I attribute solely to an infirmity of memory, by no means unusual.

Q. Was there anything noticeable in him at that time?

That was at the time, when at the age of twelve, he went from home to school and lived as an inmate of her house—

A. I do not remember anything except that he was very affectionate and very much attached to me.

She undoubtedly thought he was, and probably she had not the slightest idea that this affection was merely that of present interest, because she gave him his bread and butter and sugar, and put him to bed every night. She little thought then that there was a sleeping devil there, which, when the time should come, would nerve his strong but cowardly and trembling arm to lift an ax to strike at her in his wrath, although the overheated and faltering coward had sufficient self-control, not to redden the ax with his sister's warm blood. The same spirit was there then, that was burning within him afterwards, when he aimed the pistol, and *did not* restrain himself, because he thought it would promote his personal and private interest, and change the administration which had ignored his claims to office. She saw him at intervals, from time to time, and we find that all there is of it, is simply this, that on one occasion, this man, who, as Mr. Scoville pretended, never made a joke in his life, who was a special and peculiar Guiteau, who was honest, who was above all the rest of his honored family, a pure and religious-minded man, came to her. She says:

I do not think he told me the name of the gentleman who admitted him, but I remember distinctly his saying that they asked him three questions, and he answered two, and laughing about it as if it was a good joke that he got in so easy.

That was the introduction to the American bar, by Mr. Reed, of his present client.

Q. Did you continue to know him for some time after that, and see him daily?

That was in 1875—

A. Yes, sir; he was around the house and some of the time in *your* office.

That of his senior counsel on this trial.

She proceeds to describe his being brought back by Mr. Scoville *from the New York Tombs*, and then she says, she was rather mixed up in the dates, that while he was in Chicago after he left her house, he was *shifting around* from place to place, *as he always was.* Then she comes down to 1876:

He was very hard to get along with; that is, he was in what I call an exalted state; I have said it was a *highfalutin state*. I do not know as that expresses anything. I could not do anything with him. He was willing to do anything I wanted him to do, but he did it in such a way, as to annoy me more than if I had not asked him to do it.

You know he parted from the Oneida Community on *the labor question. He never liked work.* His ideas were grander:

Q. What else took place in 1875?—A. Well, he seemed not able to work very much, and when he was set to do anything he would be overpowered with the heat, and have to give up very soon and go into the house. That is the time that he raised the ax to me, when I requested him to do something, after he was overpowered with the heat and exhausted.

She thinks it was in 1875, but it turned out afterwards to be in 1876. She told him the butcher was coming, and she don't conceal the fact that she was angry at his refusal to make way for the butcher, and exhibited a somewhat warm temper, and picked up one of the sticks for the purpose of removing it from the path. Undoubtedly *he supposed* that she meant to use it by way of forcing him to do what she wanted, and he, coward as he is, lifted the ax to strike at his sister.

The PRISONER. *That never occurred.*

Mr. PORTER. His sister swears *it did occur*, and she is a woman of truth——

The PRISONER. She swore she might have been mistaken.

Mr. PORTER. (Interposing.) I did not hear it, or if I did, I do not recall it. She did not come into court with bloody hands, and she went out of it as she entered it, an honest and upright woman, believing what she averred, whether it was for the government or for the prisoner. For myself, *I have lifted no ax against his sister.* He did on a memorable occasion.

The PRISONER. That is false. She didn't swear *positively* that I did.

Mr. PORTER. (Reading:)

I was very much excited, and I said, "Take this boy, and take him off the place; can't have him here any longer. He will do some mischief."

That is the summary of the ax story. Let us see what further she says:

He seemed different in some respects from what he was when I had seen him last. He seemed to have more notion of doing something, and of being something in the world. He mentioned several projects that he wanted to carry out.

We come now to what in one view is very important. Mrs. Scoville had said, as you remember, that he acted curiously when she visited him at the Oneida Community. He would not talk to her; and as when he was about going to the Oneida Community she could not reason with him, so, when she visited him there, he was so possessed with the doctrines of his father and of the Oneida Community that she could not do anything with him, and she really thought he was half crazy. *But now we come to the crucial test;* here is his own sister, the only one who has really stood faithfully and devotedly by him, to save him in the hour of imminent peril. She tells you frankly and honestly how it was with him down to the time when he was thirty-five years of age.

The PRISONER. I have had a good deal of sympathy by the letters I get, sir; *the great mass of the American people are for me.*

Mr. PORTER:

The next thing I remember particularly about him was the raising of the ax: "*I had never had any thought of him before that he was not in his right mind.*"

Gentlemen, should not that end this case? Do you seriously believe this man was insane? As to the ax story, while to Mrs. Scoville it would really and naturally suggest the idea that he was partially out of his mind, to you, with the light of antecedent facts of which she knew nothing, for she was away when he, in a spirit of a dastardly coward, struck his father in the back, and when he was sitting at his own table and at a singular disadvantage——

The PRISONER. (Interjecting.) *That never happened.*

Mr. PORTER. (Continuing.) She did not know that it was the same man who, at a later date, struck one human being in the face, and that his brother and benefactor, who had befriended him. This did not occur until the year 1879. She did not then know that the same spirit which dictated the lifting of that ax, was afterwards to impel him to the direction of a more formidable and deadly weapon against the first life in the republic. It is not strange that she should have thought at that time that he was partially out of his head. But, after this cowardly and brutal assault, all through her testimony we find no act or utterance indicative of insanity. She visited him, and he visited her The tidings came to her of this culminating crime, and, faithful even unto death, she came here to defend the brother who would have cloven her skull. This lifting of the ax against his sister, in entire harmony with the depravity of the bloody-handed murderer, is the only evidence of insanity that can be raked out of this forty years, by his own devoted and faithful sister. So much for Mrs. Scoville.

The PRISONER. It was *very stupid of the Scovilles* to say anything about that ax business. That's part of *their* theory, and the prosecution are using it in a way they didn't intend it should be used. *That is about as smart as the Scoville family are.* The whole thing is bosh from beginning to end.

Mr. PORTER. We do find that in a period of forty years, after a roving life from State to State, and among multitudes of men, through the local police courts, through the various jails, through the court-rooms in which he was not a fortunate practitioner, but in which he boasted of his signal success in defending a single lawsuit and getting beaten at that, there happens to be one among all these multitudes whom he can call to prove apparent insanity, and to a certain extent there is a tendency in that direction. It was to prove *the Abrahamic order of insanity.* The primary purpose of calling this witness, who swears that he was a lawyer, and that he has been *secretly acting as counsel in this case,* though not appearing in court, was to prove the insanity of the prisoner. That witness wrote letters to or through his son, and was in doubt whether they were in his handwriting, in order to establish the fact of insanity of Guiteau. I will deal with that before I come to the other aspect of his evidence. He endeavored to impress you with the belief that Luther W. Guiteau, the father of the prisoner was insane, and would have had a defense if he had murdered the President. He gives a most excellent character the elder Guiteau, absolves him from all homicidal tendency, attests no act of delusion, and nothing inconsistent with an upright and honorable life, but says he had peculiar religious views, and one of them was a very bloody one. He tell this strange story. I do not know but there is somebody even in the jury-box who believes it. It may possibly be ; and lest somebody should credit it, I wish to read his testimony. Speaking of a certain family, this peaceable, orderly, law-abiding and religious banker said :

They ought to have all been sacrificed.

Q. You may state what he said as to the family, and if there was anything more of the conversation, state it fully ?—A. I was somewhat astonished to hear that expression from him ; but when I came to find out who it was, and what it meant, it was a family, if I remember right, by the name of Leonard P. Swett and his wife.

Dragging in, neck and heels, and without excuse, a lawyer, one of the most brilliant and most eminent members of the American bar, one who, if he had been here as counsel for the prisoner, would have controlled his client, and saved you from the levity, obscenity and blasphemy which has made the air of this Court so thick and foul; but it turns out it was not him, but somebody else.

This is the way he explained it to me.

Q. What was the boy's name?—A. That I cannot remember.

Q. Was he a son of Leonard P. Swett?—A. Not Swett, but Sweet; it was a son of Martin P. Sweet. I might state further that his idea was that all that was necessary was to believe in Jesus Christ.

Here is a man whose life stands out in the sunlight, in respect of whom we have called the foremost citizens of that town and county, men who have held the highest professional and official positions; men of character; men of weight; men associated with him in public life; men who say that he stood second to but one man, and that the celebrated and distinguished lawyer whom I have mentioned; and they all testify that the prisoner's father was eminently conspicuous for his perfect purity and integrity of character. He was not the man to be the father of a murderer. But this lawyer for Scoville and for Guiteau, this man Amerling, who does the out-door work of the cause, comes to do a little of the in-door work, and swears against a dead man, who lies moldering and mute, that the honored father of the prisoner deliberately recommended to the father and a mother of one equally dear to them to butcher their son.

You do not believe it. I do not believe it. Above all, the man who uttered it did not believe it. Let us look a little further at this man's testimony.

Again, Mr. Davidge presses him on that pretended conversation, and it is a very extraordinary one; this deliberate recommendation by a man of pure character to a father and mother to butcher their own son because he differed from them in his conviction about the propriety of going to the Oneida Community. Take this strange story a little further. Here is an incident that had been referred to in his direct examination.

"It was along about 1867 or 1868."

Said Mr. Davidge:

I don't pretend to fix the time. Witness: I will not, because I cannot do it; but there was James Cochran and L. W. Guiteau upon one side of the question and myself and Mr. Dexter Knowlton, that is now banker at Freeport, on the other side. The question was as to the taxation. I said a good deal, and the old gentleman became very angry at what I said—

This proves, as you will observe, that Luther W. Guiteau was insane—

and he pitched into me, and I, in reply, *when I had the close*, improved the opportunity and said this: I said that the old gentleman, L. W. Guiteau, was well fitted to fill all positions, but there was one he was best qualified to fill, and that was with an apron from his chin down to his toes, with a knife in his hand, in the kitchen of the Oneida Community, peeling potatoes. And the old gentleman became very angry at that.

This impudent boy, whom he had befriended; this boy whom he had helped on to fortune; this boy who had grown meantime to manhood, comes here now as associate counsel and witness, and really thinks that with a bank book showing that he had $3,000 on deposit when he left home, this jury will swallow his testimony. Gentlemen of the jury, I do not believe any one of you would think of taking your bank book with you, in order to give credit to your statements on oath, when subpœnaed in a court of justice. This is the way in which that young man, older now, and perhaps weaker, spoke in 1866 of one of the first citizens of the county in which he lived, a man with gray hair, and in an elevated and honorable position. This insult offered to that father, he says, irritated the old gentleman, and he grew very angry. Clearly the man was insane. Then he proceeds to say:

I afterwards met this man (Guiteau, the prisoner).

For once I was half inclined to believe that this lawyer told the truth.

He (the prisoner) said my life ought to have been taken from me, but God advised it otherwise, or ordered it otherwise.

This is one of the things I had forgotten, in respect of which a spark of humanity seemed to have flashed up in the prisoner's breast, but it turned out that even this was untrue, for the prisoner then said:

PRISONER: If you refer to me *it is absolutely false.*

Mr. PORTER. It is one of the peculiarities of Guiteau, that the turbulence of his bitter and intense passion has not restrained him from denouncing as a false witness, each of his own counsel who have volunteered to be sworn, and from branding as a liar the leading counsel who closed the argument in his behalf. The witness, after the denial, reasserted the fact, which he evidently thought would be beneficial to prisoner.

He was *the one* that mentioned it to me, and I afterwards talked to his father about it, and then his father said I must not mind what he said.

Let us look a little further, and we will find that this witness never saw the prisoner in his life until he came to this court-room, and the prisoner says so; and yet you perceive, how diligent associate counsel seek to supplement the defense, by thrusting forward a version of the facts, which even the prisoner confesses, against his interest, is an utter fabrication.

I pass Amerling now, and come to the curious witness North. There, too, was one who lets us into the interior history of the earlier life of the homicide, and who shows on what basis it was that Mr. Reed, simultaneously witness and counsel, gravely told you that this was a moral, a good, an upright, a Christian, a well-behaved, and a perfectly sane boy, until he went to the Oneida Community, where he was seduced and corrupted. Thomas North did know him, and his father. I propose to refer you to his evidence. It will not take much time. All this puerile mockery of North, as to Guiteau the elder, rests in the idle and fabulous pretense that he honestly believed that the father of the prisoner *thought he would never die.* The conclusive and overwhelming fact is brought out by the evidence, that the father, years before his death *insured his life,* and signed the application, which has been produced before you; and that this man, who, according to North's theory, believed he would never die, went to a lawyer six months before his death and had his *last will* and testament prepared and executed.

We have also the fabricated story, as I believe it to be, and as I think you will, in view of the circumstances of the case, that the father rejected all medical aid. It afterwards appeared, that he had attending physicians for years, physicians for his daughter, for his wife, and for himself down to the very day of his death. It is gravely and seriously claimed that the father had gone through the idle and foolish performance of kneeling at the bedside of his daughter, Flora, and commanding the unclean spirit to come out of her, and really supposed it would save her life. • Do you not think that this story would rest on better foundation, if Flora, the daughter, were here to tell it? It would not do to have Flora here. It would no more do to have her here, than to have Mr. Scoville sworn, for cross-examination might elicit disagreeable facts.

According to North's version, her father knelt by the bedside with her hands in his, and began to pray to God Almighty, and commanded the disease to leave her in the name of Christ.

So also with the other *nameless* woman, as to whom this man North testifies. If we wanted anything to enable us to characterize the witness North, could you find anything more significant than this? Mark you, he would have you believe that Luther W. Guiteau, his benefactor, the county clerk in whose office he earned his bread, and whose private roof gave him a shelter, was a lunatic. So, too, of his marvelous story of the "Cave of the Winds," as he, not being familiar with the locality, denominated it. Guiteau's father was an old gentleman, as you remember, at the time it occurred. It was in 1858. Mr. Guiteau took his clerk to Niagara Falls on a pleasure excursion. They arrived at what North calls the "Cave of the Winds." He was very impressive and oratorical on the witness stand. He described the scene, so that you saw it, like a panorama. Let us once again listen to this marvelous story, establishing beyond all controversy that Luther W. Guiteau was insane:

On the 1st of July or the 2d of July, 1858, he and I started East on a vacation trip and we stopped at Niagara Falls. We spent one day there, and hired a hack in the morning, paying five dollars for the use of it for the day, with driver.

Among other sights that we went to visit is what is called the Cave of the Winds. We went to a building to dress for that purpose in oil-cloth clothing, and when I first noticed our appearance—our shadows upon the ground—we were very much like a couple of Esquimaux Indians. We descended a perpendicular place—I forget now whether there was an elevator, or something like that—

Elevators in 1858!

or by perpendicular steps,; then we had to descend by stone steps to the mouth of the Cave of the Winds. We had a negro guide. Of course he was in advance of both of us. I was next to him, and Mr. Guiteau just behind me. We got to the mouth of the cave, and the guide had remained in behind the waterfall, and as I was in the act of doing so, I looked behind me to see where Mr. Guiteau was, and he was about, my recollection now would be, three rods behind me, and about in this attitude (illustrating by holding both hands in front on a level with the chest, about three feet apart, the palms downward)—

You remember the story, and the emphasis and mock oratory with which he told all this—

as if suddenly smitten into a marble statue—as white as marble—and there he stood, as it were, fixed in that one position. I at once returned to him.

Of course he would ; an insane man standing on the narrow edge of a precipice where descent was death ! An insane man paralyzed with terror and horror ! An insane man frozen suddenly into a marble statue, standing between the perpendicular rock behind, and the deep, whirling abyss below !

I returned to him, and as I was approaching him—

The marble statue melted ; not so far as to recede from the danger ! O, no ; the marble statue melted, only so far as to say :

"For God's sake let me alone—let me alone ; I am horror-stricken"!

What would you have done in such a case as that, if you really believed an insane man was in a position of such imminent peril ! Would you not have gone and offered him the aid of a helping hand and a strong arm, and guided him up those steps, and relieved him from a danger so appalling ? What did this man North do, according to his own account ?

I *let him alone*, and returned after my guide, and was gone from five to ten minutes behind the tremendous waterfall ; and *then* we came out and found Mr. Guiteau in the same position and attitude still.

He had traveled beneath the entire vortex of the fall of Niagara ; he had left an old man, his benefactor, whom he pretended to revere, frozen into a marble statue, and all that time Luther W. Guiteau did what would have been impossible for any other man, sane or insane, and stood in the same theatrical attitude, with both hands extended over that green and boiling abyss. North tells you he finally returned and found him *in the same position and attitude still.*

We hurried to him.

That was pretty deliberate hurrying, was it not ? Some ten minutes, he says, had elapsed. The colored guide had more humanity, supposing the man to be sane. They reached the old man.

We hurried to him and each one took him by the arm and helped him back to the building, where we dressed. He seemed to be overcome mentally.

That is where Charles got that disease of the brain, that left him the hour after he shot President Garfield—

and he seemed physicially partially helpless. We took off his oil-cloth wrappings, took our carriage, and went to the Clifton House, and there we took three things—a bath, a dinner, and a rest.

Afterwards he mentions the fourth thing—a game of ten-pins at the bowling-alley. This is the evidence that Luther W. Guiteau was an insane man. But North improves on Amerling. There is one more proof of insanity.

Q. State if you ever heard Mr. Guiteau express any sentiment akin to those which require *the slaying of an individual*, the taking of a human life ; if so, what ?

This question was very tenderly put by Mr. Scoville; for all this pretense of insanity, except as connected with the idea of the direct command of God, has been the merest sham. It was intended to give color to the part which the accused himself was to play, claiming to be under an inspiration of God. You have doubtless observed that Guiteau played as steadily into Mr. Scoville's hands, as Mr. Scoville has played into those of the prisoner, and both have been at great pains to lead you to suppose they have *two different theories* of the case. North says :

A. At an evening meeting of the circle, as it is called, a religious social circle, there was an elderly gentleman and his wife present. They had been investigating these views and these doctrines somewhat, but *they said* they had one serious family difficulty to overcome before they could join, and that that difficulty was, that they had a son *from* twenty *to* twenty-five years old, who was violently opposed to their action in the premises, and it was the source of a great deal of annoyance and a great deal of trouble to them. They went on and told their story—how their son treated them; how he talked to them—Mr. Guiteau all the time sitting there—rather leaning over in a meditative mood. At last, after they had asked the views of others, he jumped to his feet and broke out, " I will tell you what to do ; *take a knife and slay him, as Abraham did Isaac.*"

This is North's improvement on Amerling. Amerling did not venture to put in *the knife*. He was equal to the sacrifice, but not to the *Abraham*. This old gentleman, it seems had a tendency to homicidal insanity, which the prisoner inherited, and the father's propensity to shed blood was to be the prisoner's sufficient defense for deliberate and premeditated murder ! Gentlemen, there is one thing you will not fail to observe. This old man had thoroughly studied the Bible. He believed in it, and read it from day to day in his household. He reverenced it as the book of God, though he ingrafted upon it the speculative and unsound doctrines of the Oneida Community. Do you believe that this intelligent and God-fearing old man did not know what every child knows, that Abraham *did not* kill Isaac ? "Take a knife and *slay him, as Abraham did Isaac!*" Do you credit this foolish fabrication? Would it not take a thousand Norths, to make you believe that this calm, thoughtful religious old man, did really say to a father and mother, who had an only son, who did not wish to join the Oneida Community.

"Take a knife and slay him as Abraham did Isaac."

The Court then adjourned.

WEDNESDAY, *January* 25, 1882.

The Court met at 10 o'clock.

Counsel for government and accused being present.

The PRISONER. My sister has been doing some silly talk in Chicago. She means well, but she is no lawyer.

Mr. PORTER. May it please the Court: Gentleman of the jury: I have reached a portion of the argument in which the path is wearisome to me and will be still more so to you. Yet we are compelled to traverse it together. It is inevitable that there should be a dry presentation of evidence, bearing on the more material points, which tend to the exposure of the *animus* of the prisoner. I mean—and simply because I have entire confidence in you—to make it as brief as possible, to condense the few salient points of two month's of evidence within the limit of a few hours. If it be possible, I shall not even delay you one day more. My purpose had been otherwise, but admonished by this falling snow, by the changes of the season, from which I have suffered perhaps even more than you, I feel that it is of paramount importance that this trial should come to an end. If I pass hastily over some of the topics which ought to be considered, and which, if I had more time and strength, I should consider at large, it is because I rely upon your recollection of the evidence, and feel a strong assurance that you will supply any defects of mine, and penetrate to the inward truth and heart of the case. But I must, in view of the strange misrepresentations which may perchance have found a temporary lodgment in some juror's mind, refer, at least in skeleton form, to some considerations which are really controlling.

Yesterday I dropped the testimony of Thomas North, who obviously came here to aid the defense, by fixing upon his benefactor, Luther W. Guiteau, a vicarious responsibility for this murder, by transmitting his own tainted blood to the son. He left the stand, having planted, however, a quivering barb in the heart of the prisoner, when he swore to the cowardly attack on his father. You certainly will have no difficulty in reaching the conclusion that if the son is innocent now, he was guilty then, and that he was animated by a most wicked spirit, when he struck his unarmed father at a disadvantage, and fought him with the malice of a vicious and malignant fiend. That alone furnishes the evidence of a turbulent and unruly passion and egotism, which foreshadowed wrath and hate to all mankind. In his intense selfishness he lifted his hand against his only living parent, and engaged in an ignominious fight with his own father, from which he retreated with the quelled cowardice of a bully, as he afterwards evinced the like spirit by shooting the President in the back. The miserable craven fired at him, as he struck his father, from behind.

I ought to refer, gentlemen, to the testimony of John W. Guiteau. You have seen the assassin here on exhibition, as an actor, in a part, which he seriously thought would baffle the prosecution, and save him from the halter. But you now see him—as his father saw him, as his brother saw him, as his sister saw him, and came near *feeling* him and his ax. I refer to this one point of the testimony, in order that you may be reminded, in the very words of the witness, of the circumstances which, when the assassin was forty years of age, when he had fired at Garfield, when Garfield was dead, led even his own brother, *from his antecedent knowledge of his character*, to say he was sane and responsible. All that has since changed his opinion, was the admirable acting of the prisoner in his cell, and the transmission from Chicago of an old letter from his father, which he and his counsel regard as evidence of insanity, but which I regard, as I have no doubt you will, as evidence of the son's diabolical wickedness and depravity.

This brother, as you remember, is a witness, who has stood by him with the fidelity of more than a brother; who was willing to come here, and to contribute, from his somewhat limited means, all that he could to save this man's life. Yet this is the truth which he is compelled to disclose before you. I may frankly say that I believe John W. Guiteau to be an honest man. He feels naturally the bias which inclines one to save a brother's life, and to shield his own honored father's honest name, from the infamy which attaches to murder. But he is an upright man, and though his opinions under the circumstances would be no safe guide to you, the facts he states are indelible. You might just as well attempt to uproot the oak, as to uproot the conviction which this testimony must carry to your minds that, however it might have been on the second of July, *prior to that date*, he was no more insane than you or the judge, or me or his counsel. This ineffaceable fact is one which speaks to the conscience of every human being. Was his act one of depravity, wickedness, selfishness? Do you really think it sprung from a disease of the brain, curable in an hour by an act of murder. The witness says:

He called at my office.

This was in 1879. If I remember right, not three years ago—not two years before this murder.

He called at my office; he had called, I think, once before, subsequently to his having called at the house, and complained of me that I had told certain parties that he was worthless, and that they could not get his board bill, and that they had come to him and, I think, discharged him. I told him that I would not, of course, and had not, at any time, meddled with or interfered with him by any *voluntary* statements—

Such a complaint was in perfect harmony with his past career. He had made voluntary statements to and of everybody. He has made them here, to and of his honor, alternately the most fulsome flattery, and the most impious menaces. He has done the same with you. Through his counsel he has given impudent warnings to you, to whom he looks with confidence for acquittal, or, failing acquittal, disagreement. He has two tones to his voice ; he has two faces to present to the public.

One of these is masked with the sanctity of the Pharisee, and the other exhibits the hideous aspect of the fiend that possesses him. To proceed with the testimony of the prisoner's brother :

but that if any one came to me to make an inquiry about him I should simply tell the truth. He said I had *no business to make any statements* about him or his indebtedness, and that I was not any better than he was ; that I was in debt also.

As he told you from the dock :

Jesus Christ struck back, and so do I.

This is the pious and prayerful Christian. He struck back at Secretary Blaine, and asked President Garfield to remove him, under a menace, which was in due time fulfilled. He struck back at President Garfield, and, unfortunately for the nation, for the household, for the unhappy victim of his malice, for himself, he struck home. But to proceed with the reading: This, as his brother knew, unfortunately was true, and "we had some strong talk. I told him that he ought not to go to any boarding-house keeper and apply for board, without he told them or gave them to understand his exact condition."

It horrified the elder son of Luther W. Guiteau, that another son and his own brother, should be living by swindling, on the prisoner's impudent theory that "the world owed him a living"—that he had a lineal and biblical right not to pay his debts, because the Apostle Paul did not pay his—as foul and infamous a calumny as ever fell from the lips of man.

Guiteau did not live, as we are told Paul, did, in his own hired house, and while there were so many bitterly hostile to Paul, no human being except the assassin of President Garfield, has charged that the Apostle did not pay his rent. His brother proceeded:

I spoke very kindly to him, and he to me in the early part of the conversation.

So he has spoken very kindly to his honor, and kindly to you in the early stages of this trial. But does either of you doubt, that when the sentence of the law, upon your verdict, comes to be pronounced, you will hear again and again the same language of blasphemous menace, the same expressions of malignant hate, and that you will know, that if he had now the pistol he aimed at Garfield in his hand, and loaded with the same cartridges, he would, if he dared, under the plea of insane immunity, send it home to either of you, if he thought it would serve his purpose.

I spoke very kindly to him and he to me, in the early part of the conversation. I told him that, *if he was really honest*, as he claimed he was.

You see how his brother John spoke to him, long before the murder of the President. Mr. Scoville would perhaps have said, " Why, Mr. Guiteau, we all know your inborn and vital piety, know how supple your knees are, and how they are exercised morning and evening with prayer to God, how gentle and kindly your nature is, how you steadfastly imitate the divine Son of Man, and scrupulously obey His commandment, to love others as you love yourself——." If Guiteau had really loved his neighbor Garfield as he loved himself, do you believe he would have murdered him?

The PRISONER. The people I owe are *high-toned people.* I didn't go around beating *poor* people.

Mr. PORTER. (Continuing.) We have had some of them on the stand. Mr. Scoville would have said to him, No Guiteau was ever insincere. He would have told him with characteristic unction, as in effect he told you: I know you to be a man of simple-hearted and guileless truth, a man *who never jokes*, who is always mild and gentle, who is always prayerful, who always does his duty according to his pure and tender conscience, by all men. John W. Guiteau, who had known him from the time he came from his mother's womb, says to him in Boston :

If you are really honest, as you claim to be, in the publication of your book, and in your method of life, if you would go to people, and not in any way *deceive them.*

The PRISONER. (Interjecting.) I never deceived them, sir.

Mr. PORTER. (Continuing)—

and were really meritorious—

I change the third person to the first person in reading— .

you will find people very kind, even if you were unfortunate, and could not always pay your board as you agreed to do.

The PRISONER. (Interjecting.) That is right, put that in.

Mr. PORTER. There is the interior of the vile life of the prisoner. These are words spoken in perfect kindness and forbearance, by brother to brother, by a brother proud of and doing personal honor to his father's name ; by a brother who did, as the prisoner did not, remember his bright and accomplished mother. She was a pure-minded and faithful wife, who was never insane even for an hour.

Mr. PRISONER. That is so.

Mr. PORTER. That is the first tribute he has paid to the mother who nursed him, and who loved him better than he deserved.

The prisoner has introduced in evidence a hand-bill of one of his traveling lectures. Remember, this is this man who *never deceived* anybody, and who was furnishing his own recommendation of himself, and his lectures. This is in Boston :

By *the Hon.* Charles Guiteau——

The PRISONER. (Interjecting.) That is the way my letters come now always, sir.

Mr. PORTER. (Continuing.) When did he become *honorable?*

The little giant of the West.

When did this strolling humbug become "The little giant of the West?" Was there ever a more impudent charlatan? I pass this shallow pretense with no word of comment. Was he the *little giant* lecturer, I ask you? Was he not a cheat, a dead beat, and an impostor. He knows the falsehood of his impudent pretense, that the Almighty had selected him as the successor of Paul, and as a junior member of the firm of Jesus Christ & Company, to write a book, which should be an inspired sequel to the Bible, and to illustrate the golden rule, by lying in wait, in parks and alleys, and churches, and railway depots, to murder a President, who would not appoint him to a place, for which he had no qualification except strange cunning and audacity.

You remember, gentlemen, that when the prisoner was arrested in Michigan by an officer, under a law which existed in that State, by which a party coming to a boarding-place, and not paying his board, was presumptively guilty of fraud and subject to arrest, he very naturally denounced the law of Michigan as a monstrous innovation. He went in the custody of the officer, until he came to the first stopping place, at which the officer fell asleep, and then he quietly and ignominiously slipped out the car, and walked the other way twelve miles at night, and made his trail forthwith to Ohio, a State where there was no such law ; and there he made his contracts, with the printers and with the proprietors of a public hall, and was really introduced by the favor of some special interposition of Providence, by a gentleman whose name we do not learn, to an unmarried lady who desired boarders—a *high-toned* boarding-house, of course— where he for the time lived *cheap* and well, but he was disgusted with the audience he found there, and was actually reduced to what he could get, by peddling his stolen book at fifty cents a copy——

The PRISONER. (Interjecting excitedly.) That is the way the Lord wanted me to do it, and I had no alternative about it. That is the way Paul got his living.

Mr. PORTER. (Continuing.) Just listen. That was the work of *the Lord.* The Lord murdered Garfield ; Guiteau had no hand in it.

The PRISONER. (Interjecting excitedly.) Yes ; and he will murder you.

Mr. PORTER. (Continuing.) And the Lord, through this apostle, Guiteau, as he would have you believe, defrauded the landladies and the innkeepers. The Lord, as he would have you think, deceived the printers; the Lord, to whom every day before he eats, he kneels in prayer, and thanks him for his good living at other people's expense.

The PRISONER. I never *deceived* anybody about my board bill.

The WITNESS. He said at that time he did not. I am coming to that point now. He said at that time, that *he did just as Jesus Christ did.* He said that Jesus Christ went to a house, and if they received Him He blessed them, if not He cursed them. And he did just the same way.

That he was working for God, and he considered—

How convenient—

he considered that *God was responsible,* if he could not pay his board, and not him.

So when he deliberately murdered President Garfield. First, it is Blaine who is responsible; second, it is Garfield himself, who is responsible—*and for this he dies;* third, it is the Stalwarts of New York who are responsible; fourth, it is the Half-Breeds of New York who are responsible, for they misled him; fifth, it is the Democratic press and the Stalwart press that are responsible, for they wrought out the situation; sixth, it is the rebels, though, so far as I know, *they are not in rebellion.* Except by achievements in the field of war, which have given honorable distinction to men on both sides, we do not know to-day who were rebels and who were loyalists. He thought he could kindle to new life old sectional bitterness. In his, to you, closing speech, he quoted the words of a popular song, without a thought of *the utter contempt which a man like John Brown would have felt for him.* He gravely insists that this vile murder was a patriotic act; and only when he finds that all men of all parties loathe and scorn him, with a loathing and scorn absolutely unutterable, it is only then, that he falls back upon his own old resource—his vital piety. I again read from his brother's evidence:

Then we had some further conversation and I drove him to the wall, as I always did in conversation; that is, I rather attacked him; I did attack him. I entertained the same opinion of him, as he says that my father did, and I drove him to the wall. Then his spirit of antagonism would come up, and he would attempt to drive me to the wall, by asserting that I was not better than he, because I was in debt.

After awhile he *usually* intimated that he was a *fighting man.*

He has told you how eminently brave he was. The *only* evidence of that, from the beginning, is that which is furnished by his brother, and *this he denies.* Bluster has been his prominent characteristic from the beginning. Fighting, *never,* unless he could fight from behind, and, like an Indian, avail himself of the advantage of an ambush.

I told him that I *was not,* and it would be better for us to discontinue our interview, and at the time referred to, I told him that I thought he *had better leave,* and got his hat for him and *showed him to the door.* He was passing ahead of me, and he said, as he went along that I was a "*thief*" and a scoundrel."

Human nature at the best is very weak. Even John W. Guiteau, who probably never struck a man before in his life, when that wanton charge was made—that, charge which from the dock, the prisoner now admits to have been *utterly false*—before he could control the indignation which is instinctive in an honest man, slapped him on the face.

Mr. SCOVILLE. (Interposing.) Judge, he says he slapped him on the *back of the neck*.

Mr. PORTER. (Repeating.) I accept the amendment, though it does not accord with my memory. He slapped him on the *back of the neck*.

The PRISONER. (Interjecting.) He didn't hit me *at all*.

Mr. PORTER. Well, the prisoner and Mr. Scoville don't altogether agree. Mr. Scoville says he did, and that he struck him on the back of the neck.

Mr. SCOVILLE. I am merely reading from the testimony.

Mr. PORTER. Of course; the testimony has some significance to you and me, although it has none to the prisoner.

I then slapped him about as hard as that—
on the back of the neck, and he turned, and gave me one on the side of the face, which I very much respected him for. *I did not suppose he had so much pluck.*

The PRISONER. *That is not so.*

The WITNESS. I took him by the collar. This was in the office of the New York Life Insurance Company. I took him by the collar *very forcibly*.

I think either of you, gentlemen, would have put some force of grasp upon the collar of a man, who came to your office and told you impudently and falsely, as he knew, that *you were a thief*.

The PRISONER. (Interjecting.) I told him *the truth*, and I will prove it by the record, if it is necessary. Now, the point of all this kind of talk is to prove that I am a man of terrible bad temper.

Mr. PORTER. (Continuing.) What a pity, gentlemen, he has not *your* record. He claims to have *everybody's record*, and in every instance in which we have an opportunity to test it, it turns out to be a *lying record*.

I took him by the collar *very forcibly* and heartily, and *threw him down stairs*.

As the coward *went tumbling down those stairs*, the spirit of fight oozed out of him.
There they stand, *oath to oath*, the elder and the second son of Luther W. Guiteau. The younger son says, that the elder is a liar and a perjurer. The elder says that he has uttered, even though it is against the life of his brother, whom he is seeking to defend, the simple and the naked truth. *Which of these men do you believe?*

I need not refer you farther to the evidence, because you evidently remember it. No one will deny, that down to October, when John W.

Guiteau received his father's old but very significant letter, John W. Guiteau was firmly convinced that the prisoner had given himself over to the devil. This is a plain statement, founded upon the authority of *his brother's oath.*

The Prisoner. (Interjecting.) He is no brother to me. He has not been. We haven't been on speaking terms for years.

Mr. Porter. (Continuing.) It would have been better for him, if he had *never* been on speaking terms with his elder brother. He says:

I was not on speaking terms with my father, for the last fifteen years on account of that stinking Oneida Community.

If Luther W. Guiteau were a competent juror, if he were living, what would he say? You see how he condemned this wretched son for his attempt to blackmail the Oneida Community, by instituting a disgraceful and dishonest suit after he had given them a receipt in full of all demands, when all he claims, even now, is that he put in $900, of which he obtained full restitution. This old letter of his father, which they exhume, and which led John W. Guiteau, from a casual expression here, to think that *after all* he might have been mistaken, and perhaps this man was insane, speaks with eloquence and force. In enjoining upon Mrs. Scoville the necessity of that course which had led him to thrift, and a departure from which led his children, Fanny and Charles, to poverty, he says:

This thing of running in debt, especially for daily expenses, is an outrage, and one of the great causes of hard times.

Do you remember when this was written—October 31, 1875, only seven years ago—

and much of the frauds and dishonesty, that are constantly practised by many very well disposed, but unthinking sort of folks. It has been one of my own serious faults.

Referring, unquestionably, to an earlier period, when he was compelled to suspend his business as a Freeport merchant, though he afterwards honorably adjusted every outstanding debt, a trait which does not seem to have been "*hereditary.*"

It has been one of my own serious faults; it is the ruin of Wilson, *of George,* to say nothing of Charles.

For he tells you that George (Scoville) owed $100,000.

The Prisoner. (Interjecting.) If Scoville was smart, he wouldn't have put that letter in evidence. It shows what a blockhead he is.

Mr. Porter. (Continuing:)

By the way, Charles has been here for several days past; came a week ago yesterday, and remained until Thursday morning, when he took the cars to Chicago.

Gentlemen, I thought from the prisoner's statement, that for *fifteen years* they had not been even on speaking terms.

He came out here, *as it appears from his story*, thinking that through and with my aid, he could get Mr. Adams to loan him $25,000 to help to buy up the Inter-Ocean newspaper, expecting, *as he says*, to get the same amount of Charles B. Farewell; also the same amount of *a friend* who lives in New York, and the same amount of Potter Palmer, making $100,000.

The PRISONER. (Interjecting.) Yes, I knew *all those fellows;* they were good men.

Mr. PORTER. (Continuing.) You can judge from these intelligent interjections, whether he is sane or insane.

He went away very much disgusted with me, because I would not discount his note at the bank for $200. To my mind he is a fit subject for a lunatic asylum, and if I had the means to keep him I would send him to one. *for a time* at least.

Gentlemen, I am not surprised at all, that Luther W. Guiteau felt thus about that Inter-Ocean project. To him it seemed almost insane. Mr. Scoville says now it was really insane. But he has called, and we have called witnesses, who prove, that instead of being insane, it was one of the keenest and most brilliant conceptions of this man's life; and that if he had succeeded in drawing his father and friends, *who had no faith in his integrity*, into that project, with the arrangements then proposed, and afterwards carried out with Mr. Bennett of the NEW YORK HERALD, the leading independent newspaper not only in this country, but in the world to-day, it would have been a magnificent success. I speak of the New York Herald, simply because the English have taken pains to deride his honor, and the government, and all connected with this trial, for dallying with the prisoner, and not hanging him, as they recently hung a conspicuous criminal, within a month after the act of murder. Gentlemen, when England or her leading journals claim that we cannot administer justice in America; that we cannot, in the fair and orderly course of justice, convict an assassin, they belie the Court and you. Our practice is to *ascertain* guilt, before we *punish* it.

Mr. REED. (Interposing.) If the Court please, I object to that statement of Judge Porter.

Mr. PORTER. I will say nothing more on this topic, if it is disagreeable to my friend. I had supposed that no man, not even the junior counsel for the prisoner, would be unwilling, that the honor of his country should be upheld against foreign libels; but if it is otherwise, if this patriotic prisoner and his counsel are not willing to bear his country vindicated, it will be more effectually vindicated from the jury-box.

Mr. REED. If the Court please, again I object to Judge Porter's making these statements.

The DISTRICT ATTORNEY. Mr. Reed can make an exception, and Judge Porter can go on.

The COURT. I do not see that there is anything particular to object to.

Mr. REED. What I object to, your honor, is this statement of what English papers say concerning this trial. I submit that that is improper.

The COURT. It is not particularly injurious, and it is not particularly relevant.

Mr. PORTER. Suppose it were irrelevant, does any man imagine that I have not the right in argument, to use those matters of general publicity, which are known to all Christendom? Have I no right to vindicate the honor of the presiding judge, against the penny-a-liners of Great Britain. But I am content to pass the subject, without comment, and I proceed to what is not only relevant, but pregnant with significance.

This scheme, which the old gentleman thought was insane, was not only sane—it was a singularly shrewd and sagacious conception. If it could have been carried out, and *all that was wanting was confidence in his integrity*, this man instead of being in the prisoner's dock for crime, would have been a *millionaire* in Illinois, and he perfectly understands that fact. That scheme, in his hands, failed; and, simply, because among the fifty millions of people in this country, he could not find one man who would trust him, except his friend, Mr. Charles H. Reed, on whose certificate he was admitted to the bar, and *he* trusted him only to the extent of $25. A man in any matter involving financial credit, cannot, when he desires to get money, fall back on his mere fertility of brain, especially when he needs to borrow $75,000. The experience of the old gentleman, who knew the propensities of the prisoner better than we do, made him indignant, that Charles should even ask him to trust him for $200. The prisoner, however, seizes on this hasty expression:

He ought to be in a lunatic asylum, and if I could in justice to other claims upon my means and upon my family I would send him.

On this impatient expression, when the letter came to the knowledge of John W. Guiteau, he came to the conclusion, that perhaps, after all, this man might have been insane, and he reconsidered his former settled opinion. You know, what John W. Guiteau and his father did not; that the Inter-ocean project was a scheme of a strong, keen, and able man. The old gentleman goes on to say—and there you get into the interior of his heart:

His condition in my judgment has been caused *by an unsubdued will.*

Compare this, with what Mr. Reed told you of the homicide. A pure, a good, a moral, prayerful, and Christian man, until he went to the Oneida Community; and he calls it, with strange effrontery, an undisputed fact, though not established by the oath of even a single witness. His sister declares him to have been turbulent in childhood. His father punished him as, in his judgment, willfully perverse, at the age of five or six years.

It appears that when he was seventeen or eighteen, he took offense at his father, who had given him a place in his clerk's office. He struck his father, with the same hand that butchered the President, and he fought him after the blow was struck. He cringed and blubbered like a calf, when his father by a well-planted blow drew blood from his nose. It appears, too, that this filial boy, at a much earlier age, took bitter offense at his father, because he had not asked his permission to marry, after a long period of widowhood. This lordly young gentleman took such umbrage at the *undutiful* conduct of the old gentleman, that, when the father started in one direction with his wife, and left a message for his son, he started in another direction, not exactly as a deadhead, but running his father *in debt* for the money to take him to Chicago, to remain until his boasted piety should reconcile him, to *this flagrant parental disobedience* of his amiable and filial boy.

The PRISONER. (Interjecting.) I was twelve years old at the time, and I went back to my sister's house in Chicago. The conductor knew me, and *deadheaded* me.

Mr. PORTER. (Continuing.) Here we get a glimpse of the record, which could have been given you perhaps by Mr. Scoville, if he had been sworn, and perhaps not, but certainly by his sister Flora, certainly by his stepmother. Mr. Scoville was not living there it is true ; but *Flora was*, and the step-mother was. The history of those earlier years, preceding his going to the Oneida Community, *they knew*. The only material evidence we have upon that point, other than this letter, is Mrs. Scoville's, which is all discreditable to him, except the single fact that he was affectionate to her when she took care of him as a boy.

To proceed with his father's letter :

His condition, in my judgment, has been caused by *an unsubdued will*—

And that he underscores—

the very spirit of *disobedience to authority*.

A disobedient boy, a "turbulent" boy as his sister admits ; a boy who *reversed* the commandment and said, " Parents, honor and obey your children."

The very spirit of disobedience to authority and rule toward me.

You remember that he lived for most of the time with his father, until he went to Oneida, and what he speaks of here, is his conduct in the very years during which Mr. Reed presents him to you as a *model of morality*.

The PRISONER. (Interjecting.) Well, I was. *I was a model of morality* at that time, sir.

Mr. PORTER. *So Mr. Reed thinks.*

He tells you, he was obedient to the command of God in committing this murder. His father goes on to say :

Disobedient to God.

He says himself—for *he is always indorsing himself* and Mr. Scoville, except when he has occasion to think that Mr. Scoville is on the wrong tack, and then a well-prepared scene is got up, in which Mr. Scoville is denounced. He, of course, receives it meekly, with a look of mute appeal to the jury, as much as to say, "Don't you see how crazy that poor fellow is; he is denouncing even me?"

The very spirit of disobedience to authority and rule toward me, *disobedience to God and the spirit of truth.*

A liar from the beginning; and on whose authority, I presume, Mr. Scoville made his harsh and bitter assault on Mr. Edwards, a gentleman who has been for years, a trusted clerk and employee of one of the first law firms in the country—the firm of Davies, Work & Company, in the city of New York—of which the late Lyman Tremaine was a member, after he ceased to be attorney-general of New York—of which the head was the late Chief Justice Davies, who, during the progress of this trial, has closed a career of distinguished honor.

Mr. Edwards, a respectable young gentleman, trusted by such a firm, brought here by judicial process, to testify to the fact, which he happened to know, that this prisoner had in his New York office expressed his desire for public notoriety, and his admiration of Wilkes Booth; had attempted to draw the witness *into a swindling operation* for the benefit of Guiteau; had heard his boast of the fraud he perpetrated upon the Jew pawnbroker in pledging *for gold*, a watch which was *not of gold*, and the sharp device by which he escaped punishment. This witness rouses the virulence of the prisoner; and Mr. Scoville, the indorser of Guiteau, rises in due time to towering eloquence, and denounces Mr. Edwards as a deliberate perjurer. The witness swore to facts, in respect of which Guiteau was a competent witness; but Mr. Scoville did not choose to recall him to the stand to contradict them. Mr. Shaw, a respectable member of the bar, had previously sworn to the same facts, but Mr. Scoville denounces him as a perjurer. On what authority? The counsel seemed startled himself, at his bold charge of perjury, and so he proceeded to transform this witness *into a Jew*, without the slightest foundation for the allegation. Even if it had been true, I have yet to learn that it is a dishonor to any man, to be a countryman of the Redeemer of mankind, or of the lineage of that ancient people, so distinguished in the history of our race. It is no discredit to be of the same race with David, whose psalms we still sing in our churches; with Solomon, from whom we still learn wisdom; or with Abraham, the progenitor of a more than royal lineage.

The PRISONER. (Interjecting.) That is very fine, but the Lord and the Jews had a falling out at the destruction of Jerusalem, and it has followed them ever since. *The Jews are very nice people nowadays.*

Mr. PORTER. (Continuing.) Mr. Edwards is coolly *transmuted into a Jew*—by a lawyer, who did not ask his descent, and does not know where he was born—for the purposes of this case, and after the witness leaves, he *quietly proceeds to circumcise him*; a rite, which I question the authority of Mr. Scoville to administer, certainly not in the presence of the court and the jury. Possibly he might have made a stronger case of insanity, if he had whispered in his client's ear on that memorable fourth of July, "When you come to be tried for this crime, proceed to *denude yourself* in the court-room, for you have a constitutional right to be confronted with the accusing witnesses." Gentlemen, *he has stripped himself to nudity*, in a moral if not in a physical sense, as I shall show when I come to his evidence. Let us resume his father's letter:

Disobedience to authority and rule towards me, disobedience to God and the spirit of truth, which culminated in a quarrel with Mr. Noyes and the O. C.

The Oneida Community.

I do know—

And that he *underscored*, and it is evidence before you, introduced by the prisoner, and on the authority of his own father:

I do know he has in all that matter, as well as his other acts of disobedience, been *instigated by Satan*, and satanic forces; and I warn whosoever it may concern, to beware how they yield themselves to the wicked one.

There is the record of this man's insanity. I lay it down; as we would turn down and close a coffin lid. Gentlemen, when we come to the evidence of his living brother, when we come to that of his living sister, express and specific to the point, that she never suspected him of being out of his right mind until 1876; when we come to the evidence that there was a step-mother and a half-sister, whom he of course calumniates and traduces, and who of course are not here; when we produce the wife who lay side by side with him, when he would have you believe, he was a religious man kneeling by her bedside, though *she does not testify that she ever saw it*, and though, if it were true, he and his astute counsel would have been glad enough to prove it by her——

Mr. SCOVILLE. (Interposing.) If the Court please, I object to that. There is not a word of that in evidence.

Mr. PORTER. There is *this* in the case. If he had done so, and she knew it, he or his counsel would have asked her, when she was here upon the stand.

Mr. SCOVILLE. That is *another* thing.

Mr. PORTER. That is the *very* thing. The record is here. We produced her as a witness.

Mr. SCOVILLE. I am on the floor, and I have the attention of the Court. I want the record read.

Mr. Porter. I do not consent that the record be read in the midst of my argument.

Mr. Scoville. I ask that the reporter read the expression of Judge Porter.

Mr. Porter. The gentlemen may have the whole record read, if he chooses, *after* the conclusion of my argument.

The District Attorney. Let him file his objection.

The Court. (To Counsel.) Suspend until we can see what the trouble is.

Mr. Scoville. I ask the reporter to read that expression.

Mr. Porter. I object to that. I do not suppose the reporter is employed by the United States attorney, to occupy part of my time in summing up this case.

The Court. I want to see what was said.

Mr. Porter. Oh, if it is for your honor's information, it is all right.

Mr. Scoville. (to the reporter.) I wish you to read what Judge Porter said, about his not kneeling in prayer, as being in the evidence of his wife.

The Reporter. (Reading.) " When he professes to have been kneeling by her bedside, though she never saw it, or he would have been glad enough to prove it by her."

Mr. Scoville. That is what I objected to. He says that he professed to have been kneeling by her bedside and she never saw it. I say there is no such thing in evidence.

Mr. Porter. No, I did not say that. I said, in substance, as the reporter read, and as the jury heard, "He would have been glad enough to prove it by her." The counsel objected, and *we* could not examine her on this question. *They could.*

The Court. I understand that Judge Porter reaffirms now, that it is simply an inference from your omission to prove the facts.

Mr. Porter. I do not say anything different now, from what I did before. I do not, I confess, like the idea, your honor, of having it assumed that I am wrong, when I know that I am right.

The Court. Whether it is in the evidence or not, is a question for the jury.

Mr. Scoville. I desire to have an exception.

Mr. Porter. Inasmuch as it is not alleged and proved as a fact, there is no ground for the exception.

The Court. It is for the jury to decide, whether there is such evidence or not.

Mr. Scoville. Will the Court permit me an exception?

Mr. Porter. I object to the exception. He can except to the rulings of the Court. He cannot except to my argument.

The Court. I do not think there is any ground for an exception.

Mr. PORTER. Now, gentlemen, I have given you the substance of the family evidence. I stated to you, that the first question was, whether this man was insane? If he was not, that ends the case. It is only an *insane* delusion, and that of a sufficient degree of force to obliterate for the time the sense of moral or legal right and wrong, as his honor will tell you, which can shield him from responsibility. If he was not insane, there you can stop. I ought not perhaps to occupy much time with the other evidence, but I must call your attention to it. There are two witnesses, who are claimed as experts in this case, for the purpose of showing that this prisoner is insane. One of them is a Dr. Kiernan, with whose face you have become very familiar, for I think he has been here from the earliest stage of the trial. He gives an introductory account of himself. He comes here as one *experienced* in diagnosing the insane. His experience cannot be large, for it is only eight years since he was twenty-one years of age. His chief dignity was, that he was for three years *an apothecary*, dealing out medicines on the prescription of the physicians at Ward's Island. For a portion of that time he was *assistant* physician, and *he was discharged*, as he swears, for one cause, and as Dr. Macdonald, the brilliant and able President of the asylum, swears *for another*. He tells you frankly, that he does not believe in a future state of existence. He thinks men are *born insane;* that there is but a very small portion of the insane, who are in lunatic asylums; *that one-fifth of the people of this country are lunatics,* *ten million of them*. In this proportion, two of you are insane, with a fair chance of a third, the chance being fractional. Whether the learned judge happens to belong to the four-fifths, or to the one-fifth, he was not kind enough to intimate, the other judges not being here. Whether I am of the unfortunate fifth, I do not know. I think the doctor, however, would have no difficulty in certifying me to a lunatic asylum, if he could be assured, that I really think the President was assassinated by the prisoner, and not by my Stalwart friend, Colonel Corkhill. Guiteau, I presume, shares the feeling of the counsel, that the men who killed the President, are the men who are now prosecuting Guiteau, and that Mr. Davidge and I must have stood behind, with our hands in our hip-pockets, ready to shield the gallant marksman, after he had shot the President in the back. This witness evidently believes, that insanity is a condition, closely allied to idiocy or imbecility; that insanity consists in a *tendency* to visionary schemes which turn out to be *unprofitable ;* in an inability to exercise as much good judgment as common men do; and he seems to think that if any man, having those peculiarities, a tendency to unprofitable schemes, and lacking the judgment of ordinary men, were brought to him, he would unhesitatingly give a certificate, which would consign him to a lunatic asylum. Well, gentlemen, that is the effect of this evidence so far. What more? He had been here during most of this trial. He had seen the prisoner in court. I do not now remember whether he also saw him out of court.

The DISTRICT ATTORNEY. He examined him in the jail.

Mr. PORTER. He examined him in the jail; and even this man, who believes that when he dies, *it will be as the dog dies,* never to rise from the grave, and to be held to just responsibility for his acts or his words in this life; even him, they dared not ask whether he believed from that examination that Guiteau was insane.

Mr. SCOVILLE. I think you are mistaken in that.

Mr. PORTER. Well, I will gladly give way, while you turn to the testimony. It is possible I am mistaken, but I looked over the voluminous evidence with some care, and failed to observe it. *I wish you would find it.* (After examining the record.) I do not see it, Mr. Scoville. I think you must be in error. Do you find it? If you do, it will give me great pleasure to correct the error, which, I think, you erroneously impute to me.

Mr. SCOVILLE. I refer to page 747. He says that he would certainly write the case as one of hereditary insanity.

Mr. PORTER. Write what case?

Mr. SCOVILLE. This case.

Mr. PORTER. He is answering a question, as to his conclusions from *the statements of previous witnesses* as to the supposed insanity of relatives.

The DISTRICT ATTORNEY. The point was, that Judge Porter said, Mr. Scoville did not ask him the question as to the result of *his own examination of the prisoner.*

Mr. PORTER. He put to this witness the *hypothetical* question.

Mr. SCOVILLE. (After further search.) *I do not find it, Judge. It may not be here.*

Mr. DAVIDGE. I think you can assume that it is not there, Judge.

Mr. PORTER. I think it is not there, but I do not choose to have the matter left in doubt.

Mr. DAVIDGE. *It is not there.*

Mr. PORTER. So you see, gentlemen, you may leave *the results of his personal examination* out of the case, as his own counsel chose to do.

Now we come to Dr. Spitzka, of whom I intend to say nothing unkind. I do not need to do so, if I were otherwise so disposed, as I am not; for he is the friend of a valued friend of mine. If he can stand on this record, before any intelligent man who reads it, let him stand. His acquaintance with this prisoner began, I think, on a Friday or a Saturday. It lasted until Monday, when he gave his evidence.

Mr. DAVIDGE. And saw him on Sunday at the jail.

Mr. PORTER. That was his introduction and his parting, with the homicide, who shot President Garfield. You have lived with Guiteau, day by day, for two months and a half. You know him a little better than Dr.

Spitzka does. Well, the doctor tells you, what honors have been heaped upon him, honors without number, the *principal* one of which was that he once wrote a prize essay, and that he is a professor. *You remember of what sort of a college, and what sort of a professorship.* He says:

The result of my examination was that I found this man insane.

And a little below:

A moral imbecile.

Not an *intellectual* imbecile; a *moral* imbecile. *I wonder if Lucifer happened to be on trial,* what Dr. Spitzka would say of him. Would he call him, too, a moral imbecile, a moral monstrosity? Satan fell, if we may believe the record of inspiration, from the empyrean heights, and sunk to the depths, whence come those temptations which haunt man, and curse him, and doom him to punishment here and hereafter. But there was a *change* in Satan. Dr. Spitzka thinks there never was a change in this homicide. He was a moral imbecile, that is, wicked and depraved, from the beginning. *Certainly he was not a fiend, before he could talk.* Mr. Reed tells you that he had to be sent to school to learn to talk.

A *moral imbecile,* or rather *a moral monstrosity.*

I read from the record:

Mr. DAVIDGE. See if I get it down right. First, a tendency to insane delusion—

Not an insane delusion, but a *tendency* to it.

to the formation of delusive *opinions*—

Is there one man here who has not formed delusive opinions, even during the progress of this trial? When you heard Mr. Scoville open this case, did you not form opinions which have since proved to you a perfect delusion?

of morbid *projects.*

Why is the greater part of mankind poor? Because of morbid projects. Are the greater part of mankind really insane?

I should perhaps say, that the prisoner, whom I examined in your presence, has been in a more or less morbid state throughout his life, for *nothing can be more intensely morbid than a precocious and ever-growing proclivity to wickedness.*

Well, if he means a moral monstrosity, I think he makes the insanity too long, for I cannot conceive that a human being can become "a moral monstrosity" until he knows the difference between right and wrong, which most children do not know when they come—*toothless and baldheaded* into the world.

Of course, you remember, the burden is upon the homicide to prove his insanity.

On Dr. Spitzka's evidence, it is seriously insisted that the prisoner was *probably* insane on the 2d of July.

Are you prepared to find a verdict that he was *probably* insane, when the law, as expounded by the Court, requires that unless you honestly believe him to have been then *insane* it is your duty to convict him; and even if you should be led by the evidence to that conclusion, you must go to the further question of the actual *degree of insanity*. Dr. Spitzka was never in charge of any lunatic asylum. He has tried three times to obtain such a situation, *and has failed three times*, notwithstanding his prize essay, which I do not doubt was creditable to him, as a young and somewhat inexperienced theorist. I hope he may have better success hereafter. He formed an opinion, from an examination of the prisoner. He told you what the examination was, and the result is, that, in the opinion of Dr. Spitzka, he was *probably* insane. I do not think you will concur with him in that somewhat crude opinion. But it turns out, that before he ever saw the man, he had already *a fixed opinion* that he was insane, formed on newspaper statements. It was already fixed and definite. That was in the month of October, in which I landed from Europe, and having very little acquaintance with this department of psychological investigation, and being referred by a valued and eminent personal friend, to his friend Dr. Spitzka, as a young gentleman of professional skill and honor, and as a proper person to send on, in order to *ascertain* the actual mental condition of this prisoner, and having been already notified that I should send some one to make this investigation, I called on Dr. Spitzka, to know if he would undertake that task. *I had never before that day seen or heard of the man.* Do you think anybody would call him now, in any honest case? I saw him once then, and I have seen him here.

Let me read from his testimony:

Q. You say you examined the shape of his head? A. I did. Then I said to him, "I will have to know a little more about the psychology *of your crime*."

And to ascertain that he passed his hand over his head.

I found that he had the legal attainments, as far as I have a right to pass upon them, of a *third-rate shyster* of a criminal court.

Mr. Scoville can tell you what that is; I cannot.

If you were to ask me whether he knew the *legal consequences of acts*, I should say without any hesitation, that at least since he has been a lawyer, *he has always known the legal consequence of criminal acts*.

The PRISONER. *That is one of Scoville's bright witnesses.*

Mr. PORTER. (Continuing to read:)

I became convinced in my examinations of him, that the crime, for which the man stands indicted, was *the result of a morbid project rather than of a delusion*, strictly speaking. Delusive opinion entered into this crime.

Gentlemen, what do you think of announcing to the community, that if a man chooses to murder a lady, or a child, or an old man, and has a defense of not guilty interposed, and Dr. Spitzka is then called to examine the prisoner, and, testifying in behalf of the murderer, claims that the crime was the result of a *morbid project*, rather than a delusion, would you turn the man loose to murder other old men, other ladies, and other children; to fire houses, to forge bills of exchange and bank-notes; to commit midnight burglary, to stand with a pistol over the head of your wife, while the thief rifles your pocket, or carries off your pantaloons.

Mr. Davidge asks Dr. Spitzka this very pertinent and incisive question:

You concluded, then, that the shooting of the President was not the result of any insane delusion, but rather of a *tendency* of the mind of the prisoner to the formation of morbid projects?—A. Yes, that is the main motor in the case. I did not use the expression moral insanity, but some authors call that moral insanity which I term moral imbecility or moral monstrosity.

Q. You concluded that he was born a *cripple in respect to moral sense?*
A. That is about the amount of it ; correct.
Q. Well, now about his head.

You have seen the head in the plaster cast. You have seen it in the dock, as it was shaped by a power greater than that of the plasterer.

The defective innovation of the facial muscles, a symmetry of the face, and pronounced deviation of tongue to the left.

You notice, gentlemen, that the deviation of the tongue was, during the progress of this trial, and that it has constantly been, to the left, *in the direction of the jury*.

Q. Well, what sort of a head is it ?—A. That is what we term a rhombo-cephalic.

I wonder what the doctor would think of a vicious and kicking horse ; for he has pre-eminently, a rhombo-cephalic head. The owner proposes to thrash the horse, and to pass a rope over his back, to hold him down, or set him kicking at an elastic ball swinging behind him, until he is absolutely tired of kicking at anything. "Don't do that," says a surgeon, of the Dr. Spitzka school, "don't do that ; this horse has a rhombo-cephalic head. It is a case of *moral monstrosity*, otherwise called *moral insanity*. Treat the horse gently ; nurse him and pet him; don't punish him; don't shoot him." "You would not," to use the language of my friend Mr. Reed, "you would not certainly shoot 'a poor, harmless, and lunatic' horse."

There is beyond all doubt, a typical symmetry. No person's head in this room is probably exactly correspondent with any other. I am speaking now of the ideal halves of this rogue's head, not the actual mathematical halves of our own heads, which are never exactly equal.

Q. *How many heads* have you examined in reference to the increase of one side over the other ?—A. Probably *more than a thousand.*

What a busy life this young doctor has led. Just think of his examining over one thousand heads in order to arrive at the degree of deviation. He ought to have a prize for that very unprecedented feat. But now he puts in evidence something, that is really a little pertinent. It answers the odd question of Mr. Reed. Mr. Reed tells you that you are really twelve emperors, and seems to think that if one of you will, in despite of the evidence and the opinion of your fellows, set up a doubt, founded on the unproved assumption that Guiteau has a diseased brain, and that he is really and truly insane, and that he was so on the 2d of July, you can, at least, obstruct the course of justice, and add two months more to the life of this cowardly homicide, by postponing the final conviction to that extent. I am sorry to say that even Dr. Spitzka does not agree with him.

If I had only that man's face to guide me, I would say that he might be a *very depraved man* or a moral monster, *I would not know which.*

That includes the lop-sided smile; that includes his well-played wild eye. When Mr. Reed told you, that you could judge better, than those who are experienced in dealing with lunatics; that your judgment ought to override the undisputed evidence; that you, upon your own view, could decide whether a person was really insane, he gave a very curious illustration of a great historical truth. The world had lived, since the era of the French revolution, in profound ignorance of the fact, that the beautiful and brilliant Charlotte Corday was insane.

It was left for Mr. Reed, to announce the fact to this jury and this Court, for the first time in the world's history, that this splendid girl was insane. She cannot turn in her grave, but there are some of us yet alive, who know the bloody but radiant history of that extraordinary peasant girl, who, in her youth and beauty, consummated an assassination which was more than just.

The PRISONER. You would have hung her if you had been there.

Mr. PORTER. Never! She was one of the *noblesse* created by the God, whose name this prisoner blasphemes. She was no cringing coward. She left the humble house in which she was reared, to liberate France; to stay the hand of revolutionary slaughter, to lay her own head, as a cheerful and joyous offering beneath the guillotine, in order to save the effusion of blood among those, who were bound to her by the holiest ties, because she most heartily believed it her duty to the France she loved. She made her way, with calm and deliberate preparation, sane in mind, and devoted in purpose, ready to die that others might live, and she succeeded in finding access to the cold-blooded and criminal ruler of the hour, who held in his right hand the lives of millions of Frenchmen, and who, by jotting a mark of blood opposite the name of any Frenchman or Frenchwoman, could hurl his victim into that dismal dungeon, from which there was no escape, except through the iron jaws of the guillotine. She devoted herself to this holy work, caring nothing, and providing nothing, *for her own safety,* and looking to no reward from her countrymen. It was an act of patriotic self-devotion, which will warm all hearts through all after-time. It was no precedent for this cowardly and cold-blooded assassination. She laid down her life as cheerfully for her country, as Stonewall Jackson laid down his. Both acted upon an honest, even though it were a mistaken conviction of duty. Such men, such women, we all honor; but a flippant lawyer, taking the word of a murderous liar, is really convinced by *his* client, as you may fairly infer; that, when he was strolling about Washington and visiting the Corcoran Gallery — for he was studying precedents, the Lawrence case, the earlier cases of murder, the case in New York, the case of Hiscock's murder — he found Charlotte Corday, and *detected* in her beautiful face the evidences of insanity. Clearly, the assassin, or his counsel, made the discovery that the Charlotte Corday, who will live immortally in history as one ready to give her own life for her bleeding country, was really insane. Mr. Reed professes to have discovered it *in her eye*, and, forsooth, he brings forth this murderer, and places him by the side of that pure and beautiful girl, who gave her life that others might live, and seriously appeals to you to look at *this Charlotte Corday in pantaloons*, and pity him, as if he were, like her, a female martyr to a sense of patriotic duty.

Gentlemen, do you think that Charlotte Corday played the part, which in this man has so disgusted us all. When, on rising that morning, she walked out calmly, with the crucifix on her breast, to the place of execution, the world knew that hers, though a bloody, was a patriotic homicide.

You remember the gusto, with which the prisoner dwelt on the case of Wilkes Booth. I confess, though I know it will not accord with the general sentiment of the country, I have, notwithstanding my clear conviction that Wilkes Booth was a sane man, a feeling in respect of him, not that he was right, not that he had any justification, even in his own conscience, for that murder; but that there were, in his case, circumstances which tend to mitigate in some degree the horror we feel for the act of the assassin. He was a man wholly devoted to the cause which had signally failed; he looked upon Abraham Lincoln, and rightly felt that his calmness, his wisdom, his devotion, his patriotism, had been the iron bar, which had prevented the Southern States from achieving their indepedence; he had been a brilliant play-actor; he had been in the midst of many temptations, and among many evil surroundings; the heat and excitement of that bloody war had not yet passed away; the circumstances excited him; he was stimulated by the love of notoriety, which has led to so many crimes; he mingled this, with the idea of a wild and exalted patriotism; he became infatuated, not insanely, but irrationally, with the idea that he should be rendering a service to that portion of the country, with which he had cast his fortunes, if he committed the act for which he was ready to lay down his life.

The PRISONER. That is a lie, and you know it. Booth killed Lincoln from revenge, and I shot Garfield from patriotism.

Mr. PORTER. (Continuing). And so he bravely and manfully gave up his own life. Of course, neither you nor I would justify his act. It was defended, neither by the Confederate army, nor the people of the Confederate States. It was justified by no man North or South; but I cannot say that, even now, I have not some degree of commiseration for the brilliant life so unfortunately ended, by an act which, I really believe, was in some degree induced by a feeling of misguided patriotism. Are there any of the mitigating circumstances here, which attach even to the memory of the murderer of Abraham Lincoln? None. When this murderer did his bloody work, it is true he shot from behind, but he felt that he was not putting his life in peril, for he was not like Booth, in the midst of a crowded audience. Booth, with the instincts of manhood, and believing he might be justified by his Southern countrymen, leaped from the gallery to the stage, afterwards mounted his horse, rode for life or death, as it might chance, and, as it chanced, rode to death. Within the blazing flames of the building in which he was penned, as God sometimes pens murderers, he still presented the lion front of a brave man, and although maimed and crippled in body, he died like a hunted stag at bay.

The PRISONER. I shot *my man* in broad daylight.

Mr. PORTER. The President of the United States was not "my man," and this coward, this disappointed office-seeker, this malignant, diabolical, crafty, calculating, cold-blooded murderer, carefully providing death for his victim and *safety for himself*—will you seriously compare him with Wilkes Booth, who, though a misguided, was, at all events, a brave man?

Gentlemen, this man has told you of the preparations he had made for the murder. He had been making them for years. It was a contingency which he had in view, while he was in New York practicing law, in desperate circumstances, as a jail vagabond; and attorney. He was, in a narrow sense, a student. He read the popular literature of the time. He nursed in himself, that strange love of ignominious notoriety, which he admired so much in Wilkes Booth. Though warned by his landlord, Mr. Shaw, that this was a kind of notoriety, which was associated with danger and infamy, he does not seem to have profited by the admonition. Now, when he is in peril of the penalty of death, he deliberately contemplates this well-contrived pretense of inspiration or insanity, as one of the many brilliant conceptions, or *morbid projects*, as Dr. Spitzka would have called them, which opened indefinitely before him. Of course he did not believe that.

It illustrates the peculiarity of the man's mind, his wickedness, his recklessness, his depravity, that he should even think of such wild and puerile absurdities. I have had my attention called to a passage in a popular novel, which was published in 1866, in the city of Philadelphia, by the celebrated and brilliant authoress Ouida, which illustrates just the topics I am dealing with. In the course of a dialogue between two of her characters, we get a graphic illustration of this order of man. A reference had been made to a remark of Wilkes, the celebrated Englishman, who said that he was the ugliest man in England, but only fifteen minutes behind the handsomest man, as we learn from another authority. In reference to this casual remark, one of the characters in the book I have cited, which has been, since 1866, on every book-stall where popular novels are sold, says :

> Let me be the ugliest man in Europe, rather than remain in mediocrity among the medium plain faces. *There is not a hair's difference between notoriety and fame.* Be celebrated for something, and if you can't jump into a pit, like Curtius, pop yourself into a volcano, like Empedocles ; *the foolery is immortalized, just as well as a heroism, the world talks of you, that is all you want.*

The PRISONER. I don't want any one to talk about me. They talk about me too much.

Mr. PORTER. (Continuing to read.) The prisoner evidently anticipates the next sentence.

If I could not be Alexander I'd be Diogenes ; if I weren't a great hero, *I'd be the most ingenious murderer.*

This morbid and thirsty love of notoriety, has possessed this man, from the beginning. You will see that it has steadily pursued him through life, and in the end has brought him to the dock ; and it has really made him think that his name, simply because he had murdered an illustrious man, had become illustrious, and that he can send resounding down through the ages, whatever silly messages he pleases ; that he can blacken, at his pleasure, the memory of the judge, or blast even the memory of the President whom he murdered. All this is the outcome of a spirit, which we find cropping out as early as 1861, when he was a *menial* in the Oneida Community, and in his twentieth year. What had been achieved by the prisoner ? He had never earned for himself one single honest penny ; but Mr. Reed would have you believe that he was a perfect model of purity, industry, honor, religion, and morality.

In one of the sickening and maudlin letters, which he spawned from time to time, he says :

I have forsaken everything *for Christ.*

A pious, canting hypocrite, as you see, from the beginning.

Reputation, honor of men, riches, fame, worldly renown.

The boy of nineteen had *expected* all these, but he had gone to the Oneida Community, and abandoned them all *for Christ.* What a devotion to the Saviour, whom he afterwards tosses on his horn. That is his puerile and improbable story. I had marked quite a number of these curious passages in his letters, in order to refer to them. But this is enough for the purpose of illustration. This man has been all his life craving money, and procuring it as he could, by begging and borrowing devices, or by crafty, cunning, and well-considered frauds.

The PRISONER. I don't care a snap about it.

Mr. PORTER. I don't think, gentlemen, you can find two letters in that whole record, written by him, in which mention is not made of *his present need of money.* The clamor from the dock has constantly been about money.

The PRISONER. Money has been sent to me by my friends.

Mr. PORTER. The witnesses for the government, on the theory of the prisoner, are swearing *for money.* The government is prosecuting *for money.* The prisoner says:

I wouldn't have killed President Garfield, as I feel now, for *a million of dollars.*

The PRISONER. Nor for *fifty million.*

Mr. PORTER. You have heard that over and over again, until it sickens and nauseates you. He is, of course, very penitent, *with the gallows standing stiff and erect in front of him.*

Money has been this man's God from the beginning, money, and an inordinate craving for *notoriety.* The "Hon." Charles Guiteau, "The Little Giant of the West," glorifying himself by false pretenses, wherever he was, and seriously endeavoring to persuade you, that Providence wrought a miracle *in his behalf.*

The same spirit of murder which was there on the 2d of July, was there when the prisoner was an applicant for the Chilian Mission. Unfortunately for his purpose, Mr. Greeley died. There was no special intervention of Providence in that case, to give him the Chilian mission, which he asked.

Later and special interposition of Providence in his behalf is put forward, showing the same insatiate appetite for notoriety, that we have had illustrated before. It was foreshadowed by Mr. Scoville. It was a part of the preparation of the defense, but there is no human being to swear to it, except the prisoner, and he thinks that you can be swerved into the belief of that foolish story. He got, as he pretends, upon the cars one night. "*As a dead-head of the Lord;*" and he proceeded from New York to Newark, when an irreverent and unreasonable conductor, *whose place depended upon his fidelity,* came around and wanted the prisoner's fare. Well, he told the conductor, "*Charge it to the Lord;*" The conductor did not think that his charge, *without any letter of credit,* would bring the money.

So the conductor called to the brakeman, to put Guiteau off at the next station, and have him arrested; and this poor, pretended lunatic was so frightened with the horrible idea of being arrested, in a case where he and everybody knows there is no power to arrest, as for crime——

The PRISONER. (Interrupting.) There was, *in that particular case*. I would have gotten into the lockup.

MR. PORTER. He may have committed a *personal fraud*, but I know nothing of that. Mr. Scoville says he was so frightened, that "the poor lunatic," although the train was going at the rate of thirty-five miles an hour, went to the platform and leaped off, and Providence preserved him.

THE PRISONER. That is true, sir.

Mr. PORTER. It is as true as his oath, and no truer. It is as true as anything uttered by this liar from the beginning, and I do not believe either his assertion or his oath. He *felt* that it was not true, and that it was doubtful whether it would be received as truth, and so he adds a circumstance, to the effect that he had a seventy-five dollar overcoat on, and that this was lost. What? A man with a seventy-five dollar overcoat on, not ready to pledge it, in order to save himself from summary arrest?

The Court adjourned at that stage of the testimony. When we met again, you can readily imagine what took place.

The witness says:

I wish to *correct* a part of my testimony, your honor. I said yesterday that I had a seventy-five dollar overcoat. It was, but *I only paid $5 for it*.

The PRISONER. I got it at a second-hand store. I was poor at that time. The man thought I was a good fellow, and *gave it to me*.

Mr. PORTER. Why, gentlemen, if he had really been guilty of that extremity of cowardice, how much occasion for gratitude would there have been? It would have averted the sacrifice of the life of the foremost citizen of the republic. But those who jump in terror from a train, going at the rate of thirty-five miles an hour, don't come out of it with a torn overcoat or a mere scar. Yet he really has a small scar, that serves not only this *but many other purposes*. It is the scalp scar of that imaginary stone, thrown in boyhood; it is the *duplicate* scar of that fall on the New Jersey railroad ties, in which I confess I have no faith; it is the scar of that leap for life, at the peril of his seventy-five dollar overcoat. Gentlemen, remember that this is nothing, but the fabricated statement of a vile and dishonest man, for the purpose of convincing you that he is really an insane man.

You remember that of the experts whom we have called, who are competent by experience and observation, as well as a personal examination of some tens of thousands of lunatics — every one says, after personal examination of this prisoner, that beyond all doubt *he was never insane*. Of the thirteen eminent men, who swear in our behalf to that conclusion, I need only to say, that three were subpœnaed in the first instance by the prosecution, but *many more* were subpœnaed by the defendant. His witnesses came here, with the conviction that he was insane. Their judgment was very naturally based upon published rumors——

The PRISONER. (Interrupting.) They all said, I was insane on the 2d of July, and after they saw Corkhill they changed their minds.

Mr. PORTER. (Continuing.) After I cross-examined the prisoner, they all came to the conclusion that he was perfectly sane, and notified the counsel for the prisoner, that they all so believed. When the defendant's witnesses were gravely interrogated as experts, on the hypothetical question, whether *if* the prisoner was insane, he *was* insane, these experts, who came as witnesses for the defendant, agreed that upon a hypothesis, utterly unwarranted by the evidence, the prisoner *would have been* really insane. The actual fact was, that after they examined the man, they all agreed that the prisoner was sane and responsible. Some of them left; some remained.

Now, gentlemen, can there be a doubt, that these witnesses, subpœnaed for the defendant, standing as they do among the foremost men in this country; selected simply because they were foremost men, men of national and European reputation, men who are known as eminent scientists throughout the world, men to the care of whom, you or I would wish to be committed, if we were unfortunately to be stricken with this affliction of insanity — *all these men concur in the conclusion*, from their experience, and their observation, that this man had no disease of the brain—had no shadow of insanity; was as sane as any one of us. These are the witnesses; and Mr. Reed will, as he has already done, seriously appeal to some one of you "twelve emperors" to decide :

Whether you will find your verdict according to the facts, or whether you will, *as kings or emperors*, condone an unparalleled and atrocious crime.

This cold-blooded and malignant prisoner, who professed to have slept well through those thirty days—when he saw the effect of his testimony, *took it back* with most earnest promptitude, and said he couldn't sleep, and that the first good night's rest he had, was after he got in jail as the murderer of the President.

When you hear such utterances from the prisoner, do you not know that what he says is sheer and absolute imposture?

At this point the Court took a recess until 1 o'clock.

AFTER RECESS.

Mr. SCOVILLE. If it please the Court, before Judge Porter commences, I want to say a single word. I believe I interrupted Mr. Davidge only once in two days, to which I think he took exception. All I want to say, your honor, is this: I shall not interrupt the gentleman, unless I think it very necessary I should, and when I do so, I will do it in a respectful manner, and I would like to have a respectful hearing. I certainly will not interrupt him in any way, if I can avoid it, so as to disturb the current of his argument. It is not my purpose to do that. I simply want an opportunity to call the attention of the Court, in a proper manner, and in a respectful way, to any matter that may arise, without associate counsel jumping up and, before I can make my exception or make my objection, insisting that I shall not be heard. That is all I have to say about it.

Mr. PORTER. (Resuming.) I thought of your severe exhaustion, before the adjournment, and made up my mind that, no matter what might happen, I could safely intrust this case to your charge without the addition even of a single word. But I will use an hour, possibly two, certainly not more, in recalling to your attention a few of the pregnant and significant utterances of the prisoner, some on oath, some in his own handwriting, and some from the prisoner's dock; for I feel that I shall be doing you great injustice, if I should detain you one hour beyond what seems to be absolutely necessary in the concluding argument. You know me. I think I know you. I have been under your observation, and I have known you for two and a half months. I believe every man on this panel to be an upright juror, and a fair-minded representative of his countrymen. If I fail in presenting to you the leading facts in their full force, your recollection, in aid of mine, your judgment and your clear sense of right, will make up any deficiencies of mine, whether due to my comparative inexperience in the department of criminal law, or to the present infirm condition of my health; for I have shared with you, and with his honor, the Judge, a most oppressive malarial atmosphere, which none of us could avoid.

Gentlemen, there is *one man, at least,* between you and the grave of the slaughtered President, *who absolutely knows*, whether this defense is a mere sham, utterly and absolutely false, a simple imposture. I think it will only be needful for me to occupy the remaining hours of this trial *with his own declarations;* and it will be mainly, in the prisoner's language that I shall address you. These statements were not given spontaneously, as evidence of his own, of his clear and undoubted guilt. They were almost involuntarily made, in pursuance of that law of heaven, by which, "truth will out," bursting through all concealments, and opening to the light of day the actual facts, in despite of all human devices to cover them; and if it come from no other source, it will burst from the conscious and swollen heart of the criminal. I have not reduced my extracts to order, because I intended to continue my address until to-morrow, and I have not been able to formulate it. I feel, however, that the time has come, when this cause should be sent to you, and decided before this day's sun goes down. The country and the world will breathe freer for your verdict, for all humanity respects the security of human life.

I have hastily, during the intermission, glanced over, and thrown out such passages as I did not, in the present aspect of the case, care to trouble you with; and I have marked others for citation. I have not even time to arrange the order of my topics of remark; but surely I need not; for every material utterance that is to be made to you now, will come from the assassin of President Garfield. He seriously, and perhaps honestly thinks he has so *masked* this case, that your intelligence and your appreciation of the motives of human action cannot penetrate it. If I do not reduce them to methodical order, you understand the unprecedented circumstances under which I present them. They are the utterances of the man, who says he stakes his life on the act, and who says he is ready to go to the gallows *on this political issue*, and heaven forbid that you should interfere with his well-considered purpose.

Now, we have before us, the one man on earth, who can look into the depths of Guiteau's heart. This puerile testimony is given by the prisoner on oath. I asked him the plain and pertinent question in view of his creed, as a disciple of John H. Noyes:

You never had a *devilish* delusion?

If any human being in this assembly can say, that the devil never tempted him, surely it is not this prisoner. The prayer so familiar to all, contains a petition *that we be not led into temptation*, and the Divine author of that prayer knew human nature. Is there really one that is without sin? The Divine answer is, No. In the case of Guiteau, we learn, somewhat to our surprise, that the murderer of the President was *never* tempted, and "never had a devilish delusion." This New York lawyer, *alone of the human race!* This is the same man, who said, over his own signature, before he became *a liar of national reputation*, and in reference to his experience in the Oneida Community:

I see clearly, that *I have been the victim of a self-willed, self-conceited fanatical spirit*, and I hereby renounce my separation from it, and loyally yield myself to be molded by the Community spirit.

For two or three years previous to my leaving the Community, I was tormented with the conviction that I had a great mission to perform, but now I am satisfied that it was *a devilish delusion* that tormented me.

. The PRISONER. (Interjecting.) *I take that back now.*

Mr. PORTER. (Continuing.) As agile now from the dock, as he was in creed and conscience in the past. The brother and the father most firmly believed, that he had surrendered himself to the service of the devil, early in his vile and blasted life. They confirm, what he says in this letter. From a very early period in his life he was under *devilish* delusions, not *insane* delusions. This masked homicide says to you again and again: "I don't care a snap for notoriety, and never did!"

"I serve the Lord, and *he is responsible for my board charges*."

The PRISONER. (Interjecting.) Correct.

Mr. PORTER. (Continuing to read.) "I have forsaken everything for Christ." "Reputation." Certainly he forsook that. "Honor." Certainly he forsook that. "Riches." Certainly he *never* forsook wealth. "Fame." Most certainly he *never* forsook that. And "worldly renown," to attain which, in the spirit of pure diabolism, he comes here to defy to law, and to justify cold-blooded and malicious murder. I have transcribed these notes from the record, and so shall not stop to turn to the pages.

This assassination was an inspiration—what the homicide calls an inspiration. As at an earlier day, he had been *inspired* to go to the Oneida Community, as he had been afterwards inspired to leave it, as he had been inspired to establish the Theocrat, which was, as he in effect admits, literally stolen from Noyes, and to anticipate his intended publication; as he admits over his own signature; so he proceeds to his work. For whom? For the Lord, as he would have you believe. "It appears to me," as he says in his letter, "that there is a splendid chance for some one to do *a big thing for God*, for humanity, *and for himself.*" A chance to do *a big thing for Charles Julius Guiteau.*

That was the so-called inspiration. He had no ill-will to mankind. He said he never had any ill-will to mankind, or to any human being.

The PRISONER. (Interjecting.) Correct.

Mr. PORTER. (Continuing.) No, it is not correct; because he said to you, he had ill-will towards John H. Noyes——

The PRISONER. (Interjecting.) I forgot that.

Mr. PORTER. (Continuing.) And that he ought to have been hung twenty years ago.

The PRISONER. (Interjecting.) There is some little truth in that. That is the worst case I have on hand.

Mr. PORTER. (Continuing.) He says that "for 6,000 years"—now observe, gentlemen, for this has very singular significance:

For 6,000 years the world has been a school of errors. They knew not God nor Christ. Their religion—

Which was the religion of mankind.

A mere cant.

This is the man who shocked the moral ideas even of the Oneida Community.

Their *social life* is worthy only of the darkest days of Judaism.

This is his judgment upon mankind through sixty centuries, embracing, in that long line of successive generations, all there is that is honorable in the history of the human race, and recorded to-day in the divine annals, which will never be effaced. Did Voltaire ever utter so wicked a sentiment? Would Judas Iscariot if he were alive?

He was going in, as he says, to do a big thing for God and inspiration, and himself.

I claim that I am in the employ of Jesus Christ & Co.

This, gentlemen, is the reverent and prayer-making Christian; the murderer of the President, who does things, merely through the sincerity of his religious conviction, and in violation of all God's commandments. His authority to commit murder did not come to him in a vision, either by day or by night; it was not audible; it was not written or oral. It came to him in the form of *a private and personal conception*, that he had been baffled and disappointed in his claim as an office seeker; that if the Stalwart party had been in power, it would not have disappointed him. He foolishly believed, that if he could replace them in power, they would reward him. He claimed to be inspired by the Deity, and he murdered President Garfield, simply because the Deity did not think it worth while to work a miracle, in order to *convince him* that it was not, as he suspected from the beginning, *an inspiration of the devil* to assassinate the President.

To proceed with this infamous letter:

The very ablest and strongest firm in the universe, and what I can do is limited only by their power and purpose.

Again, as illustrative of the character of this man, as represented to you by his brother-in-law, Mr. Scoville.

I decided to leave the Community *clandestinely.*

Should you be so good as to loan to me, Mr. Scoville, now $50, just at this emergency, [though he does not want it, and probably would not accept it,] such an unexpected act would be appreciated, and the imaginary loan would be promptly returned.

The PRISONER. (Interjecting.) He loaned that amount to me, and I *returned it.*

Mr. PORTER. Never; except *as bait money to secure further advances.* What were the relations existing between these men, which made him, in this particular instance, fulfill his promise I do not know. I doubt whether he ever fulfilled one before, to any human being, except under some pressing and immediate necessity. What had transpired between them in the past, I do not know. But that there was something in the past which might admit of easy explanation, is indicated by the following sentence:

If the money is sent, please send me *a genuine fifty-dollar greenback,* without you can do better.

A *genuine* fifty-dollar greenback!

The PRISONER. (Interjecting.) I don't know why I put that in there. I must have been cranked badly.

Mr. PORTER. (Continuing.) The explanation does not seem to come, even now. To proceed, while the prisoner is in an apologetic mood:

Perhaps this is the place to ask *your charity* for the lack of good sense displayed in the letter, which I wrote some three or four years since.

Written, as you remember, when he was in the Oneida Community, which carries it back to 1862 or 1863.

Declining to enter into businees with you.

This so-called insane man, scarcely of age, not yet admitted to the bar, is offered by his brother-in-law, an opportunity to go into business *with him*, and here he is apologizing, for the indignant answer that he gave in declining an offer, which, in his childish vanity, he thought *ignominious*.

I take these extracts, referring to his papers, just as they happen to reach my hand, from my intelligent and valued young friend, Mr. Roth, who has been of great service to me on this wearisome trial. You will see that they all come in place.

I not only *believe in a personal devil*.

I have no doubt that is the reason, why he was so terribly frightened when Jones shot at him. But, as he says in his letter:

I not only believe in a personal devil, but I *believe in a personal God*, and when my pressure is upon me, *I test them* in that particular case.

Speaking of the murder, and the authority by which he claims to have committed it, he says :

At the end of two weeks I *discovered* that *the Deity did it.*

The PRISONER. (Interjecting.) *I did it*, and he has confirmed it.

Mr. PORTER. You see, that even in this act of blood, he assigns the *second place* to the Deity.

Proceeding with his statement :

I want to say right here, that if the *political situation* had not existed, there would have been no cause for his removal.

As I have repeatedly stated.

What ? Does he seriously assume to *answer for the Deity?* Did the Deity *explain to him* his reasons ? Did the Deity submit it to *his* judgment, foolish and finite, whether President Garfield should live or die ?

Gentlemen, you observe this mild word "Removal." This was a *political* removal. The prisoner frequented libraries. He was reading all the time. He aped the style of Napoleon, and of other great men. He chuckles over it in your presence. He tells us he is *pointed, terse and graphic.* He had evidently studied the history of Charlotte Corday. He had studied the trial of Lawrence, who had attempted the "*Removal* of President Jackson." He had studied the history of the McFarland murder in New York. He found, that keen lawyers had put the proposition, that a murder *without malice in fact,* is not a murder in law.

The PRISONER. (Interjecting.) You were one of the attorneys in that case and got beat.

Mr. PORTER. I never had any connection with the case, as counsel or otherwise. The assassin had read, as every reading man does, the works of Shakspeare. He had studied the dramatic parts, in which *villainy*, in all its phases, is portrayed by that great master.

For it was to this, Guiteau had dedicated his life. Where did he find this word "*Removal*" to soothe a troubled conscience, and soften the act of murder? It was doubtless in the study of one of the most vile characters conceived by the genius of Shakespeare, and studied, not only by those who like to know the varied developments of human nature, but especially by those, who seek in Shakspeare to learn, how in other days villany wrought its work, and *how it thrived*.

I refer to the preparations he made for the crime; for as he stole the theory of the *second advent*, and the doctrine of a *personal devil*, from Noyes—as he stole from Chandos the motto of his life, as I showed you this morning—so he stole from Shakspeare, the easy method of *smoothing over murder*, by calling it a mere "*Removal*."

I refer, first, to the second scene in the IV ACT of Othello, which contains the dialogue between the tempter Iago, and the tempted Roderigo.

Iago. Sir, there is especial commission come from Venice, to depute Cassio in Othello's place.

You remember that Roderigo sought to dishonor the bed of the Moor, and that Iago knew it.

Rod. Is that true? Why, then Othello and Desdemona return to Venice.

Iago. Oh, no; he goes into Mauritania, and takes away with him the fair Desdemona, unless his abode be lingered here by some accident; wherein none can so determinate as the "*removing*" of Cassio.

Rod. How do you mean, "*removing*" of him?

Iago. Why, by making him uncapable of Othello's place; knocking out his brains.

The seed planted soon brought forth fruit. I refer to the first scene in the fifth act.

Iago. Here, stand behind this bulk.

It was night; as it was, that night, when Guiteau dogged the President to the house of Blaine, lying in wait in the alley, to murder him.

The PRISONER. (Interjecting.) I *caught him* in broad daylight. It was a square, open, manly act. There was nothing sneaking or mean about it, sir.

Mr. PORTER. (Continuing to quote:)

Iago. Here, stand behind this bulk; straight will he come:
Wear thy good rapier bare, and *put it home*;
Quick, quick; fear nothing; I'll be at thy elbow:
It makes us, or it mars us; think on that,
And fix most firm thy resolution.

Rod. Be near at hand; I may *miscarry in't.*
Iago. Here, at thy hand; be bold, and take thy sword. [Retires.]
Rod. I have no great devotion to the deed.
Perhaps that too was "*a hot night.*"
And yet he has given me satisfying reasons.
'*Tis but a man gone:*—forth my sword; he dies.

Do you see, in the very language, in which he recounts the murder, it is a "*removal.*" In the same spirit he writes:
He has wrecked the Republican party, and *for this he dies:*
He has given me *satisfying* reasons.
True, he gave him a *chance,* as the hunter does the wolf. He wrote to him to know whether he, Guiteau, would receive the appointment. "*I wanted an answer, one way or the other.*" He warned him to remove the Secretary who had refused to appoint him to this office, *or he* and his administration would come to grief.

One word about *the oroide watch.* Mr. Scoville says it was the invention of a perjured villain. "Out of the mouths of two witnesses shall one be condemned." Two witnesses have spoken, and the prisoner dared not come back to the stand and contradict them. Here is his language.

If that testimony was a fabrication, did not the prisoner know it? If that was really a *gold* watch which he pledged, did not the prisoner know it? If it was a pure invention, what means this statement of Guiteau, in the official record?

The watch was worth $50, and *you couldn't tell it from gold.*

The PRISONER. (Interjecting.) I didn't *tell* the man it was gold. I let him be his own judge. I handed him the watch, and he fixed the value of it. *I didn't deceive him in any way.*

Mr. PORTER. (Continuing.) *Then the story is not a fabrication.* How skillful Guiteau may be, in the valuation of mock watches, in imitation of gold, I do not know. Scoville thinks, that it is not at all impossible, that a person coming into a pawnbroker's office, with a gentlemanly address and agreeable manner, presenting the card of a lawyer in the first city in the country, with references to his high-toned boarding-houses, and his splendid connections, and representing that, by misfortune, he was reduced to a condition in which it was necessary to pawn his watch, should have been able to obtain an advance of $25. But how did it happen, that after he obtained the money, he went back to his office and chuckled over it, if it was not a cheat, and an intended cheat. Again, the question has arisen here, as one of law, what constitutes criminal responsibility? The prisoner, who has devoted much attention to that subject, has admonished us that Dr. Spitzka's craneology theory is all humbug, but that *spiritology* is the key to unlock this case. He says:

Will is controlled by spirits, not by intellectual processes.

His honor will tell you, that if the will of this man was controlled by intellectual processes, as yours and mine are, and if he could do or refrain from doing a criminal act; if he could choose betwen the personal God and the personal devil; if he could elect whether to shoot or not to shoot the victim of his malice, he is guilty in law.

The PRISONER. (Interjecting.) He won't do anything of the kind, sir, under the decision of the New York Court of Appeals.

Mr. PORTER. (Continuing.) Guiteau differs materially in opinion from that learned Court.

But let us resume the reading:

I have always been a peaceable man. I don't fight with anybody, and no one fights with me. I never struck my father, and I never thought of striking him.
I don't care a snap about notoriety—not a snap.

That is a good quartette—solid: Conkling, Grant, Arthur and I.

Not, of course that he cared a snap about notoriety.

General Arthur will take care of me.
The government don't want me convicted.

The PRISONER. (Interjecting.) That is true.

Mr. PORTER. (Continuing.) The gentlemen in charge of this prosecution are Colonel Corkhill, Mr. Davidge, and myself.

The gentlemen here don't want me convicted, and I ain't going to be, probably,
I repudiate the idea of Mr. Scoville. *I am not insane now,* and never pretended that I was.

The PRISONER. (Interjecting.) On the 2d day of July, and for 30 days before that, I was insane; that was an insane act. That is what I have always said about it.

Mr. PORTER. (Continuing.) Again at page 1747:

I do not pretend that I am any more insane than you are; nor haven't been, since the firing of that shot.

The PRISONER. (Interjecting.) That is what I have always said about it, sir. It is true.

Mr. PORTER. (Continuing.) What a sudden cure of the disease of the brain!

Transitory mania is my case.

The PRISONER. (Interjecting.) You were on the case of Sickles, and got beat on the very doctrine you are trying to fool this jury with.

Mr. PORTER. (Continuing.) The prisoner, *as usual,* is mistaken. I had nothing to do with either of those cases. But Guiteau's, should be called a thunder-and-lightning order of insanity. It comes with no warning. It makes its appearance like a stroke of lightning, a flash upon the night sky.

The stroke is given, and the flash is gone. The prisoner was entirely sane *before* the flash of that June night, entirely sane *after* the stroke of the July bullet. He was the victim of *transitory mania*, as he has so often told you. Dr. Barker photographed Guiteau, although he had not examined him. He did so in such vivid colors, that if his testimony stood alone, eminent as he is as a scientist, it would hang this prisoner, when you apply to Guiteau the scientific tests, which the doctor so admirably elucidated. Let us resume the reading:

I claim transitory mania.
That is all there is of the case.

The PRISONER. (Interjecting.) *That is exactly it, sir.* That is all I claimed from the start.

Mr. PORTER. (Continuing.)

I don't claim that I am insane any more than you are, except, *on*—

Not *before*, not *after*—

on the 2d of July.

When the sun rose on the morning of the second of July, President Garfield was in the full vigor of health and life, honored and trusted, respected and beloved. When the sun went down that day, General Garfield was in the agonies of a long, slow, torturing and lingering death. A great calamity had, in the meanwhile, happened to this swindling Guiteau. When the sun rose that morning he woke from a refreshing night's sleep. He took his bath; he ate his hearty meal; he examined his bull-dog pistol, which he had bought some weeks before; he found it was in working condition; he wiped it to keep it so; he wrapped it up carefully; he arranged the papers that were to be found in his pockets after the murder; he arranged those that were to be hurried off that day by the telegraphic wire; he went to the depot; *he completed the arrangements for his own safety ;* he provided for all the contingencies that might arise. Once more, he thought he had better look at the weapon of murder; he went to a water-closet, examined it and approved it. He came out and watched the people, as they entered, unconscious of the presence of an armed murderer. He waylaid the President. *Just then*—JUST THEN, he was seized with a sudden attack of *transitory mania*, fired, fired again, and while President Garfield was swaying to the ground, he turned to find his way to that pre-engaged carriage, when he was intercepted by the policeman. *His transitory mania was gone.*

The PRISONER. (Interjecting.) I had had it for *thirty days.*

Mr. PORTER. (Continuing.) This is the insanity which he originally set up as a defense. You will remember that he claimed he was insane for thirty days from the first of June.

The Prisoner. (Interjecting.) That is correct, sir.

Mr. Porter. (Continuing.) But when he saw how that was used against him, when he discovered, by the course of the argument, that this was fatal to his theory——
He fell back on the Abrahamic theory of transitory mania, and his *last* utterance before you was one *which excluded the thirty days.* I read his words:

I don't claim that I was any more insane than you are, and *never have*, except *on the 2d of July*, 1881.

He read to the same effect in his speech, as I find in the printed report, though it did not happen to me to hear it. You did, and will remember it.

Another extract:

Now, a vast deal of rubbish has got into this case on both sides. The issue here is, *who fired that shot, the Deity or me?*

That is his statement to you, *that is his charge to this jury.* This man, who was acting under the command of Him, who wields the power of the universe, and who controls the starry system of worlds that revolve about His throne, *thinks such protection insufficient for him.* He wants Washington policemen, and General Sherman's troops, to come to the help of the Almighty against the Democrats and Half-breeds.

He did not trust the power that controls this world, and the myriads of worlds, beyond it. Why did he want help?

I knew I would be shot or hung at once, if I was not protected by the jail and the troops.

And yet this man *did not know that it was wrong to kill.*

He knew who was to be his victim, but he understood human nature well enough to feel, that whoever else might be there, they, as well as he, recognized the distinction between right and wrong, and that his only hope was in taking refuge in the sanctuary of the law, which he so recklessly violated, and finding his way to the jail, in which he sought to protect himself from the common abhorrence and indignation of mankind.

The Prisoner. (Interjecting.) I needed protection, until I could get a hearing, sir. I have got a hearing now and *people are satisfied.*

Mr. Porter. (Continuing.) Again, at page 2216:

The only insanity in this case is, what these experts call transitory mania, *i. e.*, the Abrahamic style of insanity.

He holds, you see, the Jews in a little better repute than his brother-in-law, Mr. Scoville.

They all swear I am sane now. *Nobody* ever pretended that I was not sane, *after* the shot was fired. *The insanity worked off, the moment after that shot was fired.*

On page 1065:

Did I know that I was doing wrong when I shot the President ? My answer is that *I don't care whether I knew it was wrong or not.*

The jury *do*, if the prisoner *don't.*

Mr. SCOVILLE. Will you please read the rest of that answer?

Mr. PORTER. I shall read nothing at your instance. I do not choose to have Mr. Scoville dictate my argument. Gentlemen, allow me now to recur for a moment to his formal testimony, as a witness in his own behalf. I had intended to go through it somewhat in detail. This is his answer to the following question by Mr. Scoville:

Q. I wish now to call your attention to the time and the circumstances when this *inspiration*, as you call it, first came to your mind. Where was it ?—A. It came to me one Wednesday evening—it was the Wednesday evening after Senators Conkling and Platt resigned. At that time there was great excitement in the public mind in reference to their resignation, and I felt greatly perplexed and worried about it. I will tell you about it, as far as I can. I retired about 8 o'clock that evening, greatly depressed in mind and spirit from the political situation, and I should say it was about half-past 8 before I had gone to sleep, when *an impression* came over my mind, like a flash—

You will see presently that, *if* he secured from the President the appointment to Paris, *a like inspiration came over his mind like a flash*, that Garfield would be renominated in 1884, and he wanted to assist him. But to resume :

that if the President was *out of the way*, this whole thing would be solved, and everything would go well.

I pass over a sentence that is not material.

The next morning the same *impression* came upon me with renewed force. I kept on reading the papers, with my eye on the possibility of the President's *removal—*

Evidently using that term, in the sense of Iago and Roderigo.

and *this impression* kept working upon me, grinding me, pressing me, for about two weeks. All this time I was kept *horrified ;* kept throwing it off ; did not want to give the matter any attention at all ; tried to shake it off ; but it kept growing upon me, pressing me, goading me ; so, as a matter of fact, at the end of two weeks my mind was *thoroughly fixed* as to the necessity for the President's *removal—*

That soft and tender word for murder.

and the *divinity* of the inspiration.

That is, when he himself conceived the idea, and had been for two weeks struggling to find out whether it was a devilish delusion, or a divine command, he became convinced of—his inspiration.

The PRISONER. (Interrupting.) The Deity put the idea into my mind, and *told me* to work it out as well as I could.

Mr. PORTER. Did he *tell you?* I thought you swore that you heard no voice.

Q. What was the substance of your prayer ?—A. The substance of the prayer was, that if it was *not* the Lord's will that I should remove him, that there would be some way by His providence by which he would *intercept* the act. That is always the way that *I test the Deity.*

The PRISONER. Well, he did not intercept it ; *he pressed me into it.*

Mr. PORTER. It is an excellent thing to have a man of the Guiteau sort to apply proper tests to the Deity.

When I feel the pressure upon me, to do a certain thing, and I have any doubt about it, I keep praying that the Deity may stay it in some way, *if I am wrong.*

Mr. Scoville asks him, very innocently:

Q. Did you get any intimation from the Deity whether you were right or wrong, in answer to your prayers?—A. Yes, sir ; I never had the slightest shadow on my mind as to the divinity of the act, and the necessity of it, for the good of the American people.

Mr. Scoville asks him :

Q. Where did you live during that time?—A. I lived at a first-class boarding-house.

Q. Here in Washington?—A. Yes, sir; and *had good clothes.* I was in very easy circumstances, no pressure—about money, and no anxiety about my circumstances at all.

This is the penniless swindler, who was turned away by his landlady, because he had been living at her expense, on the pretense of expected remittances.

I asked him this question on cross-examination :

You determined to kill General Garfield, did you not?—A. *I decline to answer.*

What, a man professing to be commissioned by God decline to answer?

You observe that on Mr. Scoville's examination, he swore that this inspiration came on a Wednesday night. On cross-examination he says, in reply to this question :

Do you think you do not know *when* it was, you were inspired to do this act?—A. I cannot tell you whether it was exactly two weeks or fifteen days afterward.

He has always, as it seems, had a doubt whether he was inspired on the 1st or the 2d of June. The matter of the command of God to do murder, was so immaterial, that the date did not impress itself very strongly on his recollection. Of one thing he is clear, and that is that *the command of God came two weeks after the conception by himself.*

"Q. If you made up *your* mind, it was not *his* act, was it ?—A. I say it was."

He thinks it necessary, however, to add an explanation :

I say that the Deity has confirmed the inspiration thus far, and that He will take care of me.

Q. Why were you praying to God, and professing to be in doubt? Were you in doubt?—A. *For two weeks I was in doubt*, but I have never had any doubt since that time.

That brings us to the 1st of June. Now, you will observe that he afterwards states, that *for six weeks* he was praying to God to intercept his act. When were those six weeks? If he never had a doubt after the 1st of June, whether he should commit that murder, *what was he praying about?*

A. Because *all my natural feelings were opposed to the act*, just as any man's would be.

Q. You knew it was *forbidden by human law?* A. Yes.

Q. You regarded it as murder, then? A. So called; yes, sir; so called.

The Prisoner. *I did not care a snap about it.*

Mr. Porter. (Reading:)

A. It was no matter for me, it was the Deity.

Who is this man, gentlemen, according to his own account? (Reading from page 621 :)

I have always been a peace man; naturally *very cowardly;* always kept away from any physical danger.

Again, on page 622 :

I say *the Deity killed the President, and not me.*

Then he goes on to contradict some ten or twelve witnesses, who had been sworn for the government and for him, in order that he may commend his oath to your credence—his own witnesses as well as ours. I desire to call your attention to one portion of Mr. Reed's testimony. With all his fidelity to his client, he was constrained as an honest man to swear to a striking fact, which the prisoner was quick to see, if it stood alone, might hang him.

An incident occurred, in reference to which *Mr. Reed could not be mistaken.* On the Tuesday before the assassination, he went, on account of his health, to Saratoga Springs.

Before leaving on that day, a conversation occurred between him and the prisoner.

You think—

Says the prisoner to him, at page 394—

I won't get that place, but you keep watch of the newspapers, and in a few days *you will see my name mentioned as consul to Paris.*

This is the same man who told you, that from the 1st of June, he not only would not have accepted the consulship to Paris, but would not have accepted a place in the Cabinet.

Well, this conversation came like a hard blow from Mr. Reed, but it did come.

The client told his counsel, at the time he was sworn and examined, as

I see at page 403, "*It is utterly false;*" but I think you will have no doubt of its truth.

The PRISONER. I am my own counsel here. I stand as well as Reed.

Mr. PORTER. He said on the same page.

I don't want any lying or nonsense about the defense, and I won't have it.

I will remind you of the conversation before I stop, for I see my time is getting limited. Mr. Reed says, there were two parts of that conversation. One of them related to what he would see, if he would watch the newspapers while he was gone—that he would be *appointed consul to Paris*. The *other* was this, reading from page 402:

If I *don't* get it, I will make a fuss about it in the newspapers, *or you will see my name in the newspapers;* something like that.

Of course, Mr. Reed did not understand what he was alluding to then; but he very naturally might, when the telegraphic message came to Saratoga four days afterward, announcing the shooting of the President. He understood it probably *then*, as we understand *now*, in the light of subsequent events, the memorable passage in that letter to President Garfield:

You and your administration *will come to grief.*

The DISTRICT ATTORNEY. I will read another paragraph from page 401:

He said—I should say when the conversation was about half closed, when discussing the points that the administration owed him the office, and it was due to him, that *if he did not get it, he proposed to make a fuss about it*, and that I would see his name in the newspapers.

Mr. PORTER. Now against the oath of his counsel, the prisoner plants his unsworn denial.

He explains his relations with Colonel Reed about the Paris consulship.

I asked him if he would sign it, and he said, "*Yes, he would sign it.*"

That is the application in behalf of this *insane* man, for a high official position. Then he adds:

He was the only man who actually did sign it.

The PRISONER. I expected to get position on account of my relations with Garfield and Senator Logan, and those men. During the months of March and April I stood well with them. I didn't care anything much about signatures. If you are in with those men you will be all right; if you are not you won't. This is the way. You may go there with a bushel of signatures, and it won't do any good.

Mr. PORTER. These seem to be the political ethics of Charles Guiteau, founded on his theological experience and his legal craft!

On page 648, speaking of Secretary Blaine:

I simply made the suggestion to him, that in case he assisted me in getting the Paris consulship, I should feel bound in case he was a candidate in the national convention, and I took an active part, to assist him in return. *This is the way politics are run; understand that. You tickle me and I tickle you.*

He has stated his ideas of *inspiration*, in the papers which I will read presently.

Page 652.

Q. Then there was *no inspiration* upon your part as to President Garfield's being nominated again?—A. I do not claim any inspiration on that kind of work.

On page 653 you write to President Garfield:

Q. "The idea about 1884 flashed upon me like *an inspiration.*" Was that true?— A. Yes, sir; it may have been considered so.

Strange clashing here between God's inspiration of Guiteau, to aid General Garfield to renomination in 1884, and his inspiration to murder him in July, 1881.

On page 661:

Q. Did you intend to shoot him until he was dead?—A. I intended to remove him, sir.

Q. To shoot him *until he was dead?*—A. *Yes, Sir;* I supposed one shot would do it.

Again, on the same page:

I suppose there were a thousand men in the Republican party that *would* have shot him, if I had not had the inspiration to do it.

At page 669:

The President's nomination was an act of God; his election was an act of God; his removal was an act of God.

You will remember that, for we shall have occasion to refer to it presently.

Q. Now, we came to the letter, which you say proves that you were inspired. —A. I do not say that it proves that I was inspired; I simply say that it shows the condition of my mind, to wit, that I thought it was an act of God.

Q. The President's nomination was an act of God?—A. He was nominated by the Chicago Convention.

Q. Do you think *they were inspired?*—A. I think most decidedly it was an act of God.

Q. To return to the question which the jury will want to consider. Do you think that the nomination of President Garfield was *an act of inspiration?* —

The PRISONER. Most decidedly, sir, or he would not have got it. Every one supposed it would be Grant or Blaine. They were laid aside on five minutes' notice.

Mr. PORTER. (Reading:)

A. I think most emphatically, sir, that he used the Chicago Convention to nominate General Garfield.

Q. Do you think they were *inspired?*—A. In a certain sense *I do, sir.*

Q. Do you think the *electors* who elected him were *inspired?*—A. It was not necessary that they should be, sir.

Q. Was *one of your purposes in removing the President to create a demand for your book?*—A. *Yes, sir.*

Now let us read his statements in relation to the Theocrat:

To compete with the devil, you must use the same agencies in propagating the truth that he does in propagating error, and thereby supplant evil by good. I am therefore *bold to confess—*

He is once more in the confessional—

that I should support the paper as other dailies are ; that is, by subscriptions and advertisements.

Speaking of *his former inspiration,* in his letter to the Oneida Community :

I know in my heart, that I am one with Christ and Paul and Mr. Noyes, forever and ever, and that no power in the universe can sunder us.

Gentlemen, I will not read these letters again. You remember their general tenor. This "Stalwart of the Stalwarts" tells Secretary Blaine, that if he will appoint him consul to Paris, he will support him in 1884. Failing with him, he writes to President Garfield, that he wishes he would direct the order to be made that day, appointing him to the consulship at Paris, for an *inspiration* has come upon him, that the General in 1884 will be renominated to the office.

Finally comes the assassination ; and then he writes to the American people, and to all these parties, and proclaims, "I am a Stalwart of the Stalwarts;" acting with all in turn, on his theological and political maxim " *You tickle me and I will tickle you.*"

Now, let us look for a moment, gentlemen, at these papers of his, made public on the day of the murder.

The PRISONER. Not made public, because they were suppressed by Corkhill; they ought to have been, though. They were not made public until October, when Mr. Scoville came here.

Mr. PORTER. (Reading:)

I intend to place these papers, with my revolver, in the library of the State Department.

This was one of those statements, which had been prepared, in contemplation of the murder. Does he suppose, that the Deity really wanted to have His name glorified, by having a pistol with a *white* ivory handle, rather than a pistol with a *brown* handle, deposited in the State Department, to commemorate a political assassination.

The next paper is addressed to the American press, which he thinks is so unanimously in his favor:

JUNE, 1881.

To Byron Andrews and his co-journalists:
I have just *shot* the President.

This was written before the bloody act, and he forgot to use the tender word "removed." He did not like to admit on this trial, that he even shot him; but *at that time*, he was confident of Stalwart support. He thought these men would come to his rescue, and defend, reward, and honor him.

The PRISONER. As a matter of fact they are on my side to-day.

Mr. PORTER. (Continuing.)
I have some papers for the press.

We have them here. What are they? Here is one.

WASHINGTON, *Monday, June*, 1881.
The President's nomination was an act of God.
His election was an act of God.
His removal is an act of God.
(These three specific acts of the Deity may furnish the clergy with a text.)

The clergy who were engaged in preaching a gospel, which he denounced a sham and an imposition.

I am clear in *my* purpose to remove the President.

I thought it was the *Deity*, who was clear in his purpose to remove the President; but it seems not.

I read some of the marked passages:

I am clear in my purpose to remove the President. It will save the Republic, and *create a demand for my book.*
In order to attract public attention, *the book needs the notice the President's removal will give it.*

You observe this man never loved *notoriety*. "He did not care a snap for it."

I was an applicant for the Paris consulship. I presume I should have got it—

This was to cover over the fact, that he was a disappointed office-seeker, and to prepare for his vindication afterwards—
as General Logan favored my appointment—

General Logan swears *it is not true*—

and the President seemed to favor it—

It is because he did *not* seem to favor it, that he died—

and agreed to leave it with Mr. Blaine.

So far as appears, the President never saw Guiteau in his life, never down even to the hour of his death. He had seen the President, but the

President never saw him, and *has yet to look for the first time* upon the face of the man who murdered him.

Who conceived the idea of murdering the President? Here is the answer of the prisoner, made public on the day of the assassination:

To the American people:

I *conceived* the idea of removing the President, four weeks ago. Not a soul knew of my purpose. *I conceived the idea myself*, and kept it to myself. I read the newspapers carefully, for and against the administration, and gradually the conviction settled on me that the President's removal was a political necessity.

Why? Because God commanded it? No.

Because he proved a traitor to the men that made him, and thereby imperiled the life of the Republic.

Then, again:

In the President's madness, he has wrecked the once grand old Republican party, and *for this he dies.*

The murder was not in execution of the *judgment of God*, but of the *judgment of Guiteau*, the baffled applicant for the Paris consulship.

It will make *my friend* Arthur.

What sort of *a friend* President Arthur is of his, you may infer from the manner in which you heard him reviled the other day, by this prisoner's brother-in-law.

The PRISONER. He did not represent me, sir, any more in that matter than he has in this case.

Mr. PORTER. (Reading.)

I have sacrificed *only one.*

That is all Cain sacrificed. That is all Wilkes Booth sacrificed. There are very few men in an organized society, who are permitted by their fellow-citizens to murder more than one. Only one; but when Jones shot at "only one," the thing produced a very different impression upon this theological gentleman.

I leave my justification—

Says the lofty patriot—

To God and the American people.

The PRISONER. That is what I did, and they have justified it, too.

Mr. PORTER. Is it not strange that he had *forgotten that God had commanded him to do it?* Again:

JUNE 18, 1881.

I intended to remove the President this morning at the depot, as he took the cars for Long Branch; but Mrs. Garfield looked so thin, and clung so tenderly to the President's arm, *my heart failed me to part them.*

Remember, he was under direct command of God. What did he do

I decided to take him *alone*.

As yet, we do not find the divine commandment, or the new-born inspiration.

Again, on the morning of the murder, he writes :

WASHINGTON, July 2, 1881.
To the White House:
The President's tragic death was a sad necessity, but it will unite the Republican party and save the Republic. *Life is a fleeting dream*, and it matters little when one goes. *A human life is of small value.*

Did you ever see a more desperate fight for a human life, than this criminal has made for the last two months?

He seems to have altered his mind. With President Garfield, human life was of small value, but with this man, who looks only to be removed *to paradise*, for he is a Christian man, and tells you he is in the service of the firm of Jesus Christ & Co., a human life seems to be of *considerable* value. (Reading.)

I presume the President was a Christian, and that he will be happier in paradise than here.

Strange that the same rule don't apply to Guiteau, when Mason and Jones shot at him.

I had no *ill-will* towards the President.

Don't you think he had some *good-will* towards Charles Guiteau?

Suppose that I should deliberately fire a pistol into a crowd, and imperil a hundred human lives, and should set up as a defense, that I had no ill-will either to the crowd, or the particular man I shot; the law would imply malice, and the most reckless and deadly malice.

Again reading :
To General Sherman:
I have just shot the President.
I shot him several times, as I wished him to go as easily as possible. His death was a *political* necessity.

Not only was it *not true, that it was God's act*. This letter to General Sherman puts his defense on the distinct ground, that his death was a *political* necessity. So in the letter to the White House he says :

I had no ill-will towards the President.

That was on his shallow theory of "no malice, no murder."

Gentlemen, I desire to call your attention to the testimony of Mr. Brooks. But it is fresh in your remembrance. That night, there was no pretense that God commanded the act. On the contrary, the mruderer stated to Brooks on the night of the second of July, that he acted *on political considerations*, and he stated what they were. Detective Brooks said, "Did you think you could do such a thing as a Christian man? I am a Christian man, too. Did you take God into account?"

He said he had done *his duty* to God and to the American people.

But the inspiration, the commandment of God, all this he had forgotten. When Brooks testified, the prisoner admitted that he had stated the facts as they were; so there is no doubt, the act was one of *political murder.* I come now to the testimony of General Reynolds, which I need not refer to in detail, as my time is limited. The prisoner, as you remember, admitted that the facts as stated by Reynolds, were substantially true.

He asked General Reynolds:

Where were you on the day of the assassination?

Assassination! I thought it was a removal.

The PRISONER. *I never used the word "assassination,"* sir; and Reynolds lies when he says so.

Mr. PORTER. I understood him to say, that Reynolds's testimony was substantially true. We will see presently whether the prisoner used the word "assassination" or not. It was alluded to by him first, by asking:

Where were you on the day of the assassination?
I am going to have the Harpers publish my life, my address, and my book (The Truth) all in one book. It will make about six or eight hundred pages. The Herald is friendly to Conkling, and will be friendly to me, when all this matter gets before the people, and they know just why I *assassinated* the President.

Again on page 1102 the word is repeated, and again on page 1104:

If I had not seen that the President was doing great wrong to the Stalwarts, and was wrecking the Republican party, I would not have *assassinated* him.

By the way, you should remember that this occurred, when he had been not merely a disappointed office-seeker, but a *disappointed President murderer.* At that time, it was supposed that President Garfield would recover. The prisoner had, up to that time, expected that he would die, and this would make General Arthur President. This was an unexpected reverse to him. How could the Stalwarts help him *now.* The President was alive.

He had his plan of defense, and had put it before the American people. If he had succeeded in killing the President, the Stalwarts would have been reinstated in power. But he learned from General Reynolds that *he had failed.* What was he to do then? He was very naturally startled. His original defense—that there was no malice in the act, that it was purely patriotic—would not now avail him. Still he put that forward, making the best of it he could.

"Thou shalt not kill" is written in the divine word, but probably then, the dim and crude idea occurred to him of a personal inspiration to kill the President of the United States.

The PRISONER. There are 38 commandments in the Bible, to kill for the good of the people, when the rulers did wrong.

Mr. PORTER. Did he say that *then?* Was he really "a stalwart" student of the Bible? Does he now mean to say, that it was an act of *Biblical* inspiration? Not a word of it. He had *forgotten* his inspiration then, but he remembered and claimed that it was a *patriotic* act. (Reading :)

I thought my friends would come and see me, by the hundred.
They will come when Garfield is dead. It is proper they should not come *now*.

That was the substance of the conversation. Then comes the *third* interview, when the slips were shown to him *of interviews* with the great Stalwart statesmen, as to Garfield's murder, and the burning and eloquent denunciation of Senator Conkling. Then came the letters of Senator Conkling and others, which fixed upon this murderer a brand, almost as indelible as that which the Almighty himself planted upon the brow of Cain.

The PRISONER. That is false. *They said that,* on the second and third of July. *These men are my friends to-day.*

Mr. PORTER. (Reading :)

When I told him about the President, he seemed very much disappointed. For some time, he appeared in great agony, and paced the room for a time, and then, after a little, he collected himself ; he commenced giving utterance ; after he read them, he used the words "*most astounding,*" the only words he uttered for some little time.

Then pacing the room for a short time, he became somewhat more calm, and he said *to himself,* that is, not addressing any one, "That is why : they know why." Then looking at me, and addressing me directly, "What does it mean ? *I would have staked my life that they would defend me.*"

They pretend to see only the bloody act of *an assassin.* They did want General Garfield removed. They talked about impeaching him. Then, after a pause, he said, "They raise this terrible cry against me, *for fear blame might attach to them.* They know how bitterly they denounced him."

Again, as General Reynolds proceeds to read from his notes, the prisoner adds :

He is stating what I said ; it is correct in substance.

Then, he adds :

The Stalwarts are horrified out of their senses, for fear they will be suspected. Do they know, I have stated that I had *no accomplices?* My reply was, "They do know." "And they still talk this way ?" My answer was, "*They do.*" Then the words, "*Most astounding, most astounding.*"

Then looking at the paper, and reading that extract about General Logan, he said, "The idea of General Logan saying I am insane. *I am not more insane than he is.*"

Then, after thinking for a few moments, catching the fresh idea, "this will redound to my advantage;" and then, he immediately asked for a pen and paper, and wrote hurriedly, this address to the American people. The address *is in his own handwriting.* He tells you now, that he never called his act *an assassination. This paper has never been brought to the notice of the public until now.* At the time it was put in evidence, being addressed to the American people and to the public, it was *supposed* to have been one of those published just after the assassination ; but this paper, and the other, are those written by him on the 18th and 19th of July.

I read only the material parts, because the clock admonishes me that I must soon close:

To the American people :
I was almost stupefied when I discovered the fact—

That is, that his stenographic statements had not been published ; they had been very properly kept by the officers of the government, with a view to his conviction of the crime—

> I claim that the reason the people feel as they do, is because I have had no defense.
> *I now wish to state distinctly, why I attempted to remove the President.*

Now, surely, we will at last be *reminded of God's command.*

I had read the newspapers, for and against the administration, very carefully for two months, before *I conceived the idea* of removing him. Gradually, *as the result of reading the newspapers,* the idea settled on me, that if the President were removed it would unite the two factions of the Republican party, and therefore save the government from going into the hands of the ex-rebels.

I had none but the best feelings toward the President personally. I had *no malice* and no *murderous* intent. I acted *solely* for the good of the American people. I appreciate all the religious sentiment and horror, connected with the *attempted* removal of the President. No one can surpass me in this ; but *I put away all sentiment,* and did *my duty* to God and the American people.

I claim to be a gentleman and a Christian, and do not dissipate in any way.

All my papers have been suppressed, and the public sees nothing but the fact of *the assassination.*

That is his record, made in blood, and *by the same hand* that held the murderous weapon against the life of the President, and he says *he never used the word assassination.*

> *It was my own conception and execution.*

Gentlemen, who shot Garfield ; the Deity, or this assassin ?

> *It was my own conception, and execution, and whether right or wrong, I take the consequences.*

Gentlemen, the time has come when I must close. The government has presented the case before you, without fear, favor, or affection. We have endeavored to discharge our responsible duties as well as we could, and his honor has most certainly discharged his as well as he could, under many difficulties and embarrassments *unprecedented in our judicial annals.* I know you will be faithful to your oaths, and will discharge your still greater responsibilities with equal fidelity. So discharge them, that so far as depends on your action, a least, *political assassination* shall find no sanction, to make it a precedent in our future history. He who has ordained that human life shall be shielded by human laws from human crime, presides over your deliberations, and the verdict which shall be given or withheld to-day, will be recorded where we are all to meet. I trust that verdict *will be prompt*, that it will represent the dignity and majesty of the law, your integrity and the honor of the country, and that this trial, which has so deeply interested all the nations of the earth, may result in a warning, to reach all lands, *that assassination must not be used as a means of promoting party ends or political revolution.* I trust that the time may come, in consequence of the attention which has been drawn by the circumstances of this crime and this trial, to a peril common to every well ordered and organized society, when, by international arrangement between the various government of Christendom, the law shall be so strengthened, *that the political assassin shall find no refuge on the face of the earth.* The plotting murderer who slaughtered President Garfield, knew that, against the laws of God and man, he was breaking with bloody hands into the house of life. He did not know, that over his own grave, if grave he is to have, will be written by the general consent of mankind, in dark letters, an inscription appropriate to the grave of a coward, an ingrate, a swindler, and an assassin.

The notoriety which he has sought, will be found in that inscription. He did not know, what we do, that even though by a lingering death the President yielded up his life, the hand that aimed that pistol at his back, if I may be permitted to borrow an illustration from the Attorney-General, on the occasion to which I have referred, of the dedication of the memorial statue of Alexander Hamilton, in some respects akin to this in its reminders, the asssassin unconsciously wrote the name of James A. Garfield in characters of light upon the firmament, there to remain as radiant and enduring as if every letter were traced in living stars.

www.ingramcontent.com/pod-product-compliance
Lightning Source LLC
Chambersburg PA
CBHW030902170426
43193CB00009BA/711